5A: Animals

Learn about realism.

Graeme Smith

PUBLISHED ON AMAZON.com
by
LABYRINTH BOOKS

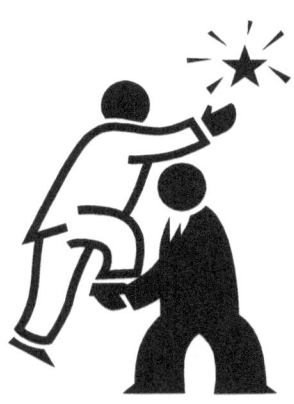

DEDICATION:

This book is dedicated to my family.
Hele-ly (Ly).
> my wife:

Ingrid.
> our daughter:

Marie.
> my former wife:

Fiona, Natalie and Michael
> our children:

Georgie
> Michael's wife:

Pearl, Kiki and Martha.
> their children:

They have put up with me for many years and I thank them for that.
I hope this book gives an insight into what occupied me much of the time.
All have done worthwhile and interesting things in the absence of my help.
I congratulate them for their achievements.

SUPPORT:

Support the International Artist magazine
– **contact:** editor@internationalartist.com

Support the Australian Artist magazine
– **contact:** editor@australianartist.com

HOW TO USE THIS BOOK.

Usually people don't think through things to the level they need to.
Because of that, they have projects instead of tasks on their "to do" list.
That leads to procrastination because it hasn't been broken down to a task level.
So go through your book once to understand it then go through it again.

Start at the PART of the book that you think you should start at.
Make notes of the steps you will need to take and the resources required.
Use the notes to make a step by step system to implement the particular ideas.
You don't have to refer back to the original, if you've created YOUR system.

The first question you have to ask and answer is "Why is this being done?"
How does this align with where you want to get to?
What are the strategic implications of doing this?
Does this fit in with getting to your goal in the shortest and fastest amount of time?
What would it be like if it were totally successful?
Define it - what is success for this project and how will you know?

Now brainstorm all the tasks are involved.
It's important not to go linear too fast, step 1, step 2, step 3, and step 4.
You end up cutting off options.
As you plan step 1, 2, and 3, there is a specific step that might be number 4.
If you start steps too quickly, other ways of doing 1, 2 and 3 may not appear.

The first 1/3 of a brainstorming session is easy - just generate lots of ideas.
The second third is a little bit more challenging.
Go through those ideas and see where they lead to.
Then push yourself to think outside the box for that's often where the big idea is!
That's where the most powerful way of getting the project done the fastest – is.

Most never get to that level and so end up short-changing themselves.
Then their project takes longer and they also set themselves up to procrastinate.
This final brainstorming part of the equation is incredibly important.

Once you fully brainstorm a project put your options into a linear sequence.
Then you can figure out what you've overlooked and everything becomes obvious.
Get your tasks in order, add missing steps, and lay out your task list for the project.

Organize tasks into a linear process and decide what things can you start immediately?
Step one is to start with no dependency on things that have to occur before them.
There might be step 5 or 6 or 20 that don't rely on anything else to get done.
You can get started on them right away!

Write what you think of at the time and also cross off things as you do them.
Add in stuff that is relevant from time to time.

As a basis for learning about realism use photographs.

Focus on learning what you can.
Action with materials = technique.
Practiced techniques = skill.
Habitual technique + skill = style.

Continue with the subject matter you want to paint really well.
That way you are continuing down the correct path (for you).
Your focus is always on portraits, landscapes, the sea, or whatever you like.

Don't just select animals focus on one (tiger, cat, horse).
Then even from the start you can become a specialist.
Also focus on something you are interested in.
This will help maintain the necessary motivation while you learn.
Over time you will develop the individual painting skills needed.
You will also know how to paint your subject your way.

Eventually you can focus on another subject.
If it is related to your original theme you will learn much quicker.
From one breed of dog to another is an example.
Then from one kind of animal to another.

You'll note the similarities and also the differences.
You could even progress from portraits to head and shoulders studies.
Later these might be full figures.

Follow this pattern for long enough, and you'll be able to paint anything!
People who do things well also do them faster than those who don't.
It's one of the indicators of skill that applies to painting just as much as anything else.

By now you should notice that repetition helps skill development.
Several small paintings are better for learning.
Larger ones take more time and that's how you apply what you have learnt.

Skill in art, sport or even medicine is basically the same phenomenon.
It's practiced behaviour in action.

Most artists don't do anywhere near enough to develop any real skill.

INDEX: ANIMALS.

ANIMALS

Learn about realism using photographs (at least to start with).
Any photograph is of something.
Instead of selecting random subject matter select the kind you'd like to paint.

An artist who lived in California wanted to learn how to paint polar bears.
In addition his painting skills were quite modest.
I suggested he do many small experimental studies by looking at photographs.
It didn't matter if they're finished or not as they're ways of learning about bears.

After 250 studies he did his first painting with no polar bear or photo.
He was totally surprised at how well his polar bear turned out.
Also the standard of the work was infinitely better than it had been in the past.
He had internalized his learning.
The polar bears he created were not any photographer's either.
They were his!

If you want to learn to paint animals, then choose animal photographs.
Like the Californian artist don't select any animal focus on one (tiger, cat).

Then even from the start you can become a specialist.
You understand the animal and over time develop the paining skills needed.
You will also know how to paint your subject your way.

Eventually you can focus on another subject.
If it is related to your original theme you will learn much quicker.
For example one breed of dog to another or from one kind of animal to another.

You'll note the similarities and also the differences.
Progress from portraits to head and shoulders studies and then full figures.

Follow this pattern for long enough, and you'll be able to paint anything!

People who do anything well also do it faster than those who don't.
That applies to painting like anything else, it's one of the indicators of skill.
Skill in art, sport or even medicine is basically the same phenomenon.
It's practiced behaviour in action.
Most artists don't do anywhere near enough paintings to develop any real skill.
Many small experiments will beat one or two major efforts every time.

But you must do the 'hard yards'!
Painting a large number of experiments develops skill, and also attitude.
You'll become more discerning, because you acquire more experience.
You'll not need, nor want, other people's assessments.

Work on a number of experiments at the same to increase productivity.
For you reduce wasted time.
Once you run into a dead-end with a painting move to another for a fresh start.
The initial painting is returned to with a different attitude, or set it aside again.

Working on a number of paintings at the same time also saves materials.
A particular colour can be applied to the work for which it was intended.
BUT there will be other works where that same colour will be appropriate.
When you buy paint, buy in quantity, but only use as needed.

Can't remember what you did previously go with what you think of now.
In the end it doesn't matter!
Usually you'll find most works will finish fresh and roughly about the same time.

Avoid major works.
They take time (years), are usually done slowly and often large and complex.
You'll tend to labour over them as you seek to do your best.

You learn to paint by painting.
You do not learn by someone telling you what to do.
That way you learn they know what to do and if you get stuck ask them.

But you can also learn by looking.
That's how you learn about the appearance of things.
Traditional art learning is based on looking and putting.
It's possible to learn many simple things and gradually combine them.
A problem is that you can only paint what you can see.
But by actually painting such things you get to understand their appearance.
You also develop skill at depicting those you do most.

Let your experiments evolve.
Those that don't work won't matter for you learn a great deal from the 'failures'.
You'll learn what to do and what not to do next time.

Regard these as exercises or studies or experiments.
They are never going to be framed, sold or kept for posterity.
Just do many and do them reasonably quickly.

The Magic Multiple Miniatures is where you can't make a mistake.
Just find out how they turn out.
It's a discovery process rather than reproducing something.

This is particularly useful when you are observing fleeting moments.
Sometimes they'll turn out great, but at other times not so.
But you don't need to be brave for there is no risk.

Do enough fleeting experiments and they WILL get better!
You will be able to capture in paint moments of life.
They've the spontaneity that is often lacking in a photographic based artwork.

Let's say you want to learn to paint dogs?
Then paint dogs not figures BUT do NOT worry about how they turn out.

Just paint them and in time they'll improve.
Maybe you don't believe this?

Years ago I trialed an art education program in an elementary school.
The art teaching was very closely linked to the materials issued to the pupils.
The particular material combinations chosen were not random.
They were designed to introduce some quite specific experiences to the pupils.
But the challenge was to see what they'd create with any given combination.
One teacher noticed a particular boy over a series of lessons.
In the earliest lessons there were always two blobs present in the work.
It didn't matter what he was given by the teacher.
Over a period of time these blobs gradually changed into two birds.
They were just basic symbol-type birds, such as most people might do.

As the lessons continued the birds improved.
There were more details and eventually became recognizable as budgerigars.
The teacher realized the boy did budgerigars no matter what material he got.
He tried to find a combination of materials that couldn't become budgerigars.

The boy always found a way to make the birds.
One time he even pin-pricked budgerigars onto paper.
Could this kid might become the best budgerigar artist in the world?
If he continued, I'd say every chance.

Why did he do this?
Well the teacher discovered (surprise) he had two pet budgerigars.
They meant more to this boy than anything else.
Because the teacher DIDN'T tell him what to do.
He could express his feelings and knowledge.
He also got much better at it!

That's how it should be learning to paint anything you want.
Just do them for they'll improve provided the motivation is strong enough.
It's also how you can develop confidence!

Imagine and learn new ways.

The artist, during the act of creating a work is expressing something.
Expression is a unique personal action.

Three artists attempt to paint the same subject, exactly as seen.

They will finish with three different works.

The differences can be attributed to the various artists' expression.

Their works are symbols for this expression.

Expression is related to emotion.

Although the individual may not be conscious of what that emotion is.

The presence of emotion creates a tension (a feeling).

Tension isn't necessarily the emotion, but an awareness of an emotional state.

Expression is bringing into perceptual form symbols for that awareness.

It is thus related to that the underlying emotional state.

The expressive act is not necessarily related to any particular audience.

There's a difference between arousing emotion in an audience.

That is intended, manipulative and a form of communication.

A similar arousal can be the result of expression.

Such expression denotes and belongs to an individual.

It is actually a characteristic of individuals.

It's not a form of communication but observers are often mistaken.

There's a difference in expressing emotion and symptoms of emotion.

The first is necessary for artistic activity and a personal reaction to a stimulus.

Symptoms of emotion are what an observer sees.

They may be manipulation of appropriate symbols without emotion (actor).

The relationship between an artist and the work is thus a personal one.

It's linked to the inner state of the artist prior to, and during, creating.

That may ultimately be a work of art.

It doesn't really matter what you do at the start.
The most important thing is to actually do something.
Let's see what happens here when I do this?

Random starts do not necessarily have to be the case.
You can plan your starts.
But take your time.
Don't rush enjoy the experience and see what you can find out.

Once you begin, you can alter or change what you have done.
It's better to do something and be wrong, than do nothing.
Mistakes can be corrected, and you learn what not to do at the same time.
Any experiment does not even have to be finished!

In the process you'll discover whatever you find out.
More importantly the discoveries are yours.
They're part of an experience rather than just part of following instructions.

Your knowledge grows from your own experiences.
This is what real learning is about.
Experience and confidence grows for the more you do the better you'll get!

You are the judge of quality, which is a variable that changes over time.
You probably have old works that you thought were excellent at the time done.
What are they like now?

1. This is the final step to being the artist you want to be.
There are seven GROUPS of experiments to help that transition.

Each group is divided into three pathways.
The focus is on the transition from experimenting to becoming an artist.
Once you have done the hard yards this is an easy and natural step.

The first follows the REALISM path.
This continues from the previous pattern of experiments.
The focus is photographs and pictures as a basis for a search for reality.

The second pathway is based on OBSERVATION.
This focus is a more traditional approach.
But the foundation has been laid with the MMM experiments.

The third pathway is linked to your IMAGINATION.
This focus is more personal.
But again there is a foundation from the MMM experiments.

Perhaps you want to try them all?
Follow the sequence of MMM experiments as outlined a logical progression.

You can follow either or both the Realism and Imagination pathways.
If your MMM focus is NOT observable.
You could follow just one of the pathways?

What if your MMM focus is not be one of those template Groups!
That's not really a problem - select the one that's closest.
For example if your focus is on fairies choose the People Group.
Then substitute fairies for people when creating your MMM experiments.

But your focus is quite different – say World War 1 military aircraft?
There's no group anything like that.
Just select a group and substitute your focus for whatever is already there.

Your MMM experiments are like the athletes training program.
As an Olympic athlete who wants to remain at the highest level - keep training.
Your MMM experiments become a normal routine.
So you need to construct YOUR OWN MMM experimental programs.
By now this should not be difficult.

Then training never stops.
Perhaps start each day with a short period of experiments.
Then move to your main artistic tasks.

2. By actually painting you understand how to do what you want to do!

There's no other way for you learn by doing.
You do not learn by someone telling you what to do.
Then you learn that they know what to do and if you get stuck you can ask.

By now you should have an experimental attitude.
You are scientific about your art learning so set yourself challenges.
See what happens here when you do this?

Magic Multiple Miniature experiments can be copied a number of times.
Then you can compare different experiments with the same image.
This highlights learning that would otherwise take much longer.

Use ONE MMM experiment as a template for a series of explorations.
Use the same materials in different combinations (black, grays, white).
Use different materials entirely (pencil, felt pen).

DIFFERENT MMM experiments as a basis for a series of explorations.
Use the same element combinations (black, grays) on each one.
Use the same materials each time (pencil, felt pen, paint).

Explore further according to your curiosity.
For example an MMM experiment could be printed on gray or coloured paper.
You could even distort the MMM image!

Don't worry about whether you are doing the experiments correctly.
Do something, it's certain to be right and also you'll discover what you find out.

Once you begin, you can alter or change what you have done.
It's better to do something and be wrong, than do nothing.
Mistakes can be corrected, and you learn what not to do at the same time.
An experiment does not even have to be finished!
Your knowledge grows from your own experiences which is real learning.

Most importantly any discoveries are yours.

They're part of your experience rather than just part of following instructions.

Your experience and confidence grows for the more you do the better you get!

Random starts do not necessarily have to be the case.

You can plan your starts but take your time.

Don't rush enjoy the experience and see what you can find out.

ANIMAL REALISM.

Photographs are a basis for learning about realism.
Any photograph is of something.

Continue with the subject matter you want to paint really well.
Then you are continuing down the correct path (for you).
Your focus is always on portraits, landscapes, the sea, or whatever you fancy.

Like the Californian artist don't select any animal focus on one (cat).
Then even from the start you can become a specialist.
You will also focus on something you are interested in.
This will help maintain the necessary motivation while you learn.

You get to understand your animal or whatever you choose.
Over time you will develop the individual paining skills needed.
You will also know how to paint your subject your way.

Move from a general focus to a narrower one.
Instead of horses you focus on race horses, or equestrian or children's ponies.
You'll note the similarities and also the differences.
Because they are all horses you will learn much quicker.

Eventually you can focus on another subject.
You'll note the similarities and also the differences there too.
Because they are related to your original theme you will learn much quicker.
Then from one kind of animal to another.
Follow this pattern for long enough, and you'll be able to paint anything!

People who do things well also do them faster than those who don't.
That applies to painting like anything else for it's one of the indicators of skill.

By now you should notice repetition helps your own skill development.
Skill in art, sport or even medicine is basically the same phenomenon.
It's practiced behaviour in action.
Most artists don't do anywhere near enough to develop real skill.

Work on a number of experiments at a time increases productivity.
For you reduce wasted time.
If you run into a dead-end with one painting move to another for a fresh start.
The first painting is returned to with a different attitude, or set it aside again.
Usually you'll find most works will finish fresh and roughly about the same time.

Working on a number of paintings at the same time also saves materials.
A particular colour can be applied to the experiment for which it was intended.
BUT there are bound to be others where that same colour will be appropriate.
When you buy paint, buy in quantity, but only use as needed.

Focus on learning what you can.
Action with materials = technique.
Practiced techniques = skill.
Habitual technique + skill = style.

NOW START: ANIMAL REALISM.

FIRST Experience Unit:

UNIT 1: Experiment 1
Copy or photocopy or print out a black and white MMM image you have chosen.
Materials:
Your choice of non-paint, opaque or transparent paint (black and white).
Brush (if using paint).
Begin:
Paint the MMM image in black and white.
Match the original tones.
Notice the shape of the animal.
Conclude:
Clean up.

UNIT 1: Experiment 2
Copy or photocopy or print out a black and white MMM image you have chosen.
Materials:
Your choice of non-paint, opaque or transparent paint.
Brush (if using paint), white paper (small).
Begin:
Copy the animal from your MMM image.
Preliminary drawing in thin paint.
Establish overall shape of the animal.
Keep the painting broad.
Then:
Use a bigger brush with black and white
Notice the shape of the animal.
Conclude:
Clean up.

UNIT 1: Experiment 3

Copy or photocopy or print out a black and white MMM image you have chosen.

Materials:

Your choice of non-paint, opaque or transparent paint (black and white).

Large brush (if using paint), white paper (small).

Begin:

Copy the animal from your MMM image.

Preliminary drawing in thin paint.

Establish overall shape of the animal.

Keep the painting broad.

Then:

Use a bigger brush with black and white

Change from the original tones.

Notice the shape of the animal.

Conclude:

Clean up.

UNIT 1: Experiment 4

Copy or photocopy or print out a coloured MMM image you have chosen.

Materials:

Your choice of non-paint, opaque or transparent paint (black and white).

Large brush (if using paint), white paper (small).

Begin:

Copy the animal from your MMM image.

Preliminary drawing in thin paint with brush.

Block in darkest and lightest areas with thin paint.

Establish overall shape of the animal keeping the painting simple and broad.

Check the relationships between the different areas.

Establish positions of head, body, legs, tail relative to each other.

Then:

Use a bigger brush with black and white

Copy the original tones.

Conclude:

Clean up.

UNIT 1: Experiment 5

Copy or photocopy or print out a coloured MMM image you have chosen.

Materials:

Your choice of non-paint, opaque or transparent paint (dark and light).

Large brush (if using paint), white paper (small).

Begin:

Copy the animal from your MMM image.

Preliminary drawing in thin paint with brush.

Block in darkest and lightest areas with thin paint.

Establish overall shape of the animal.

Keep the painting simple and broad.

Check the relationships between the different areas.

Establish positions of head, body, legs, tail relative to each other.

Then use a bigger brush with dark and light paint

Copy the original tones.

Conclude:

Clean up.

UNIT 1: Experiment 6

Copy or photocopy or print out a coloured MMM image you have chosen.

Materials:

Your choice of non-paint, opaque or transparent paint (dark and light).

Large brush (if using paint), toned or coloured paper (small).

Begin:

Copy the animal from your MMM image.

Preliminary drawing in thin paint with brush.

Block in darkest and lightest areas with thin paint.

Establish overall shape of the animal keeping the painting simple and broad.

Check the relationships between the different areas.

Establish positions of head, body, legs, tail relative to each other.

Then use a bigger brush with dark and light paint

Copy the original tones.

Conclude:

Clean up.

Further thoughts:

Copy other images of animals.

Use dark and light paint (or non-paint).

Establish overall shape of the animal.

Keep the painting simple and broad.

Check the relationships between the different areas.

Establish positions of head, body, legs, tail relative to each other.

Note the spaces in between these areas.

SECOND Experience Unit:

UNIT 2: Experiment 1
Modify copy or photocopy or print a specific MMM image you have chosen in colour.
Materials:
Your choice of non-paint, opaque or transparent paint (dark and light).
Large brush (if using paint), toned or coloured paper (small).
Begin:
Copy an animal from your MMM image.
Preliminary drawing in thin paint with brush.
Block in darkest and lightest areas with thin paint.
Establish overall shape of the animal.
Keep the painting simple and broad.
Check the relationships between the different areas.
Establish positions of head, body, legs, tail relative to each other.
Then:
Use a bigger brush with dark and light paint
Copy the original tones.
Conclude:
Clean up.

UNIT 2: Experiment 2

A specific coloured MMM image if possible taken by you.

Materials:

Your choice of non-paint, opaque or transparent paint (dark and light + a local colour).

Local colour is the approximate colour of things (black cat, brown dog).

Large brush (if using paint), white paper (small).

Begin:

Copy animal from your MMM image.

Preliminary drawing in thin paint with brush.

Block in darkest and lightest areas with thin paint.

Establish overall shape of the animal.

Keep the painting simple and broad.

Check the relationships between the different areas

Establish positions of head, body, legs, tail relative to each other.

Then:

Use a bigger brush with dark and light paint to show the original tones.

Use more dark and light paint to show form and shape.

Use the other colour to add local (as in the animal) colour.

This only needs to approximate the animal colour.

Do NOT overwork the experiment.

Many details you know are there may not be shown

Conclude:

Clean up.

UNIT 2: Experiment 3

Coloured MMM image used in the previous experiment.

Materials:

Your choice of non-paint, opaque or transparent paint (dark and light + a local colour).

Large brush (if using paint), white paper (small).

Begin:

Copy animal from your MMM image.

Preliminary drawing in thin paint with brush.

Block in darkest and lightest areas with thin paint.

Establish overall shape of the animal.

Keep the painting simple and broad.

Check the relationships between the different areas.

Establish positions of head, body, legs, tail relative to each other.

Note the spaces in between.

Then:

Use dark and light paint to show the original tones.

Use more dark and light paint to show form and shape.

Add local (as in the animal) colour.

This only needs to approximate the animal colour.

Do NOT overwork the experiment.

Many details you know are there may not be shown.

Conclude:

Clean up.

UNIT 2: Experiment 4

Coloured MMM image used in the previous experiment.

Materials:

Your choice of non-paint, opaque or transparent paint (dark and light + a local colour).

Large brush (if using paint), white toned or coloured paper (small).

Begin:

Copy animal from your MMM image.

Preliminary drawing in thin paint with brush.

Block in darkest and lightest areas with thin paint.

Establish overall shape of the animal keeping the painting simple and broad.

Check the relationships between the different areas.

Establish positions of head, body, legs, tail relative to each other.

Note the spaces in between.

Then:

Use dark and light paint to show the original tones.

Use more dark and light paint to show form and shape.

Add local (as in the animal) colour although this only needs to approximate the animal colour.

Develop your experiment but do NOT overwork it.

Gradually modify the tones and colours.

Many details may not be shown.

Conclude:

Clean up.

UNIT 2: Experiment 5

Coloured MMM image used in the previous experiment.

Materials:

Your choice of non-paint, opaque or transparent paint (dark and light + a warm and cool colour).

Two brushes (if using paint), white toned or coloured paper (a little larger).

Begin:

Copy animal from your MMM image.

Preliminary drawing in thin paint with brush.

Block in darkest and lightest areas with thin paint.

Establish overall shape of the animal keeping the painting simple and broad.

Check the relationships between the different areas.

Establish positions of head, body, legs, tail relative to each other.

Note the spaces in between.

Then:

Use dark and light paint to show the original tones.

Use more dark and light paint to show form and shape.

Add local (as in the animal) colour which only needs to approximate the animal colour.

Develop your experiment but do NOT overwork it.

Gradually modify the tones and colours.

Use warm and cool colours to show depth.

Many details may not be shown.

Conclude:

Clean up.

UNIT 2: Experiment 6

Coloured MMM image used in the previous experiment.

Materials:

Your choice of non-paint, opaque or transparent paint (dark and light + a warm and cool colour).

Two brushes (if using paint), white toned or coloured paper (a little larger).

Begin:

Copy animal from your MMM image.

Preliminary drawing in thin paint with brush.

Block in darkest and lightest areas with thin paint.

Establish overall shape of the animal keeping the painting simple and broad.

Check the relationships between the different areas.

Establish positions of head, body, legs, tail relative to each other - note the spaces in between.

Then:

Use dark and light paint to show the original tones.

Use more dark and light paint to show form and shape.

Add local (as in the animal) colour which only needs to approximate the animal colour.

Develop your experiment but do NOT overwork it.

Gradually modify the tones and colours.

Use warm and cool colours to show depth.

Many details may not be shown.

Conclude:

Clean up.

Further thoughts:

Use other photographs you have taken to explore other views.

THIRD Experience Unit:

UNIT 3: Experiment 1
Modify copy or photocopy or print out a specific coloured MMM image from memory.
Materials:
Your choice of non-paint, opaque or transparent paint (dark and light also is warm and cool).
A brush (if using paint), white toned or coloured paper (a little larger).
Begin:
Copy animal from your MMM image in dark and light areas with thin paint.
Match original tones.
Use the dark and light colours to show animal form.
Use warm and cool colour to show depth.
Check the relationships between the different areas.
Establish positions of head, body, legs, tail relative to each other.
Note the spaces in between.
Then:
Add local (as in the animal) colour.
This only needs to approximate the animal colour.
Develop your experiment but do NOT overwork it.
Gradually modify the tones and colours.
Conclude:
Clean up.

UNIT 3: Experiment 2

Memory of a specific coloured MMM image if possible taken by yourself.

Materials:

Your choice of non-paint, opaque or transparent paint (dark, light also warm / cool + local colour).

Two brushes (if using paint), white toned or coloured paper (a little larger).

A piece of glass.

Begin:

Trace animal image onto glass.

Copy animal from your glass tracing in dark and light areas with thin paint.

Match original tones.

Use the dark and light colours to show animal form.

Use warm and cool colour to show depth.

Check the relationships between the different areas.

Establish positions of head, body, legs, tail relative to each other.

Note the spaces in between.

Then:

Add local (as in the animal) colour.

This only needs to approximate the animal colour

Develop your experiment but do NOT overwork it.

Gradually modify the tones and colours.

Conclude:

Clean up.

UNIT 3: Experiment 3

Memory of a specific coloured MMM image used in the previous experiment.

Materials:

Your choice of non-paint, opaque or transparent paint (dark, light also warm / cool + local colour).

Two brushes (if using paint), white toned or coloured paper (a little larger).

A tracing glass.

Begin:

Trace animal image onto glass.

Copy animal from your glass tracing in dark and light areas with thin paint.

Match original tones.

Check the relationships between the different areas.

Establish positions of head, body, legs, tail relative to each other.

Note the spaces in between.

Then:

Use the dark and light colours but vary from the original tones.

Use the dark and light colours to show animal form.

Add local (as in the animal) colour.

This only needs to approximate the animal colour.

Develop your experiment but do NOT overwork it.

Gradually modify the tones and colours.

Use warm and cool colour to show depth.

Conclude:

Clean up.

UNIT 3: Experiment 4

Memory of a specific coloured MMM image used in the previous experiment.

Materials:

Your choice of non-paint, opaque or transparent paint (dark, light also warm / cool + local colour).

Two brushes (if using paint), white toned or coloured paper (a little larger).

A tracing glass.

Begin:

Trace animal image onto glass.

Copy animal from your glass tracing in dark and light areas with thin paint.

Match original tones.

Check the relationships between the different areas.

Establish positions of head, body, legs, tail relative to each other.

Note the spaces in between.

Then:

Use the dark and light colours but vary from the or ginal tones.

Use the dark and light colours to show animal form.

Add local (as in the animal) colour which only needs to approximate the animal colour.

Develop your experiment but do NOT overwork it.

Gradually modify the tones and colours and using warm and cool colour to show depth.

Do not attempt too much detail - only paint what can be seen by a viewer.

Conclude:

Clean up.

UNIT 3: Experiment 5

Memory of a specific coloured MMM image used in the previous experiment.

Materials:

Your choice of non-paint, opaque or transparent paint (dark, light also warm / cool + local colour).

Two brushes (if using paint), white toned or coloured paper (a little larger).

A tracing glass.

Begin:

Trace animal image onto glass.

Copy animal from your glass tracing in dark and light areas with thin paint.

Match original tones.

Check the relationships between the different areas.

Establish positions of head, body, legs, tail relative to each other.

Note the spaces in between.

Then:

Use the dark and light colours but vary from the original tones.

Use the dark and light colours to show animal form.

Add local (as in the animal) colour.

This only needs to approximate the animal colour.

Develop your experiment but do NOT overwork it.

Gradually modify the tones and colours.

Use soft and hard edges for modelling.

Boundaries between shapes should not always be too sharp or clear cut.

A soft irregular transition is required from time to time.

Gradually modify tones and colours – for example use warm and cool colour to show depth.

Suggest texture by dry-brush or sgraffito techniques.

Thicker paint may be required to do that.

Do not attempt too much detail - only paint what can be seen by a viewer.

Conclude:

Clean up.

UNIT3: Experiment 6

Memory of a specific coloured MMM image used in the previous experiment.

Materials:

Your choice of non-paint, opaque or transparent paint (dark, light also warm / cool + local colour).

Two brushes (if using paint), white toned or coloured paper (a little larger).

A tracing glass.

Begin:

Trace animal image onto glass.

Copy animal from your glass tracing in dark and l ght areas with thin paint.

Match original tones.

Check the relationships between the different areas.

Establish positions of head, body, legs, tail relative to each other.

Note the spaces in between.

Then:

Use the dark and light colours but vary from the criginal tones.

Use the dark and light colours to show animal form.

Add local (as in the animal) colour which only needs to approximate the animal colour.

Develop your experiment but do NOT overwork it.

Gradually modify the tones and colours.

Use soft and hard edges for modelling.

Boundaries between shapes should not always be too sharp or clear cut.

A soft irregular transition is required from time to time.

Gradually modify tones and colours – for example use warm and cool colour to show depth.

Suggest texture by dry-brush or sgraffito techniques.

Thicker paint may be required to do that.

Do not attempt too much detail - only paint what can be seen by a viewer.

Conclude:

Clean up.

Further thoughts:

Use memories of other photographs you have taken to explore other views.

DEVELOPMENT: Extensions

In the Development extension activities:

Draw on what you have learnt.

You can link what you have learned to your own goals.

DEVELOPMENT: Extension 1

Copy or photocopy or print out the MMM image you have chosen.

Materials:

Use the SAME materials as used in a previous experiment from Unit One.

Use the SAME MMM image as used in a previous experiment Unit One.

Begin:

BUT repeat only one of the experiments.

DEVELOPMENT: Extension 2

Modify copy or photocopy or print out of the MMM image you have chosen.

Materials:

Use the SAME materials as used in a previous experiment from Unit Two.

Use the SAME MMM image as used in a previous experiment Unit Two.

Begin:

BUT repeat only one of the experiments.

DEVELOPMENT: Extension 3

Modify copy or photocopy or print the MMM image you have chosen from memory.

Materials:

Use the SAME materials as used in a previous experiment from Unit Three.

Use the SAME MMM image as used in a previous experiment Unit Three.

Begin:

BUT repeat only one of the experiments.

CONGRATULATIONS.

The second pathway is based on OBSERVATION.

This focus is a more traditional approach but the foundation has been laid.

If your MMM focus is **NOT** observable go to the **IMAGINATION** pathway.

The focus is more personal but there's a foundation from MMM experiments.

OBSERVED ANIMALS.

Continue with the subject matter you want to paint really well.
Your focus is always on animals.

Like the Californian artist don't just select any animal but focus on one.
Then even from the start you can become a specialist.
You will also focus on something you are interested in.
This will help maintain the necessary motivation while you learn.

But now observe your chosen painting focus.
This means you are limited to things you can actually look at.

You get to understand your animal.
Over time you will develop the individual paining skills needed.
You will also know how to paint your subject your way.

Move from a general focus to a narrower one.
Instead of horses you focus on race horses, or equestrian or children's ponies.
You'll note the similarities and also the differences.
Because they are all horses you will learn much quicker.

You could progress from portraits to head and shoulders to full animals.
Follow this pattern for long enough, and you'll be able to paint anything!

Make notes, do sketches and record what you can see.
This is material you can draw on when continuing your MMM experiments.
Make a habit of carrying a sketchpad or scraps of paper and a pen or pencil.

Set up MMM experiments right where your observation focus is.
The Impressionists popularized painting outdoors.
A still life arrangement is an alternative.
To fit with your focus a sleeping pet might be as close as you can get to that.

Your observation helps you understand your animal.
Over time you will develop the individual paining skills needed.
You will also know how to paint your subject your way.

Eventually you can focus on another subject.
If it is related to your original theme you will learn much quicker.
From one breed of dog to another is an example.
Then from one kind of animal to another.

People who do things well also do them faster than those who don't.
That applies to painting just as much as anything else.
It's one of the indicators of skill.

By now you should notice that repetition helps your skill development.
Skill in art, sport or even medicine is basically the same phenomenon.
It's practiced behaviour in action.
Most artists don't do anywhere near enough to develop real skill.

Work on several experiments at the same time increases productivity.
For you reduce wasted time.
Run into a dead-end with one painting move to another for a fresh start.
When the initial painting is returned to, there's a different attitude.
If not set it aside again.
Usually you'll find most works will finish fresh and roughly about the same time.

Working on a number of paintings at the same time also saves materials.
A particular colour can be applied to the experiment for which it was intended.
BUT there are bound to be others where that same colour will be appropriate.
When you buy paint, buy in quantity, but only use as needed.

Avoid major works.
They take time (years), usually done slowly and are often large and complex.
You'll tend to labour over them as you try to do your best.

Instead occasionally do a slightly larger experiment.

Focus on learning what you can.
Action with materials = technique.
Practiced techniques = skill.
Habitual technique + skill = style.

Do you have a sketchbook?

You are probably familiar with a sketchbook.
Any old book you like, just as long as you write, scribble, draw, or make notes.
It doesn't really matter whether it has lines or the pages are blank.

It'll be full of your ideas, or memory aids for ideas in most cases.
Naturally ideas for paintings will be there.
Writing thoughts is a powerful way to commit them to your memory bank.
Then they are accessible later.
Looking at pages in your sketchbook a later date will refresh those ideas.
That will go beyond what is merely recorded in your book.
By writing your ideas down you build a bridge between what you see and actions you can take.

Do you plan effectively?
Your sketchbook can be where you start your planning.
Sometimes this will be repetitive, as minor variations are tested.
But they have to be worked through to find out what happens.
Effective planning is the beginnings of effective actions.
Your plans are the test runs for the real world.
Plans by themselves don't make anything happen, but they ease the way.
Your preparation can be quite systematic!

How will you get the most from your sketchbook?
You'll always get more from what you draw or write than what you read or hear.
Carry out sensible ideas there's a chance you'll improve on your past efforts.

If you do not try anything then there is no chance of an improvement at all.

This is particularly useful when you are observing fleeting moments.
Sometimes they'll turn out great, but at other times not so.
But you don't need to be brave for there is no risk.

Do enough fleeting experiments and they WILL get better!
You will be able to capture in paint passing moments of life.
They'll have the spontaneity that is lacking in a photographic based artwork.

NOW START: OBSERVED ANIMALS 1.

FIRST Experience Unit:

UNIT 1: Experiment 1
Start with an MMM animal observation.
Materials:
Your choice of (dark, light also warm / cool) non-paint, opaque or transparent paint.
Two brushes (if using paint), white toned or coloured paper (a little larger).
Begin:
Copy animal from your MMM observation.
Use thin paint (large brush).
Only show what is necessary.
Then:
Use the dark and light colours to show animal form.
Use thin paint before using thick paint and paint smaller parts later.
Boundaries between shapes should not always be too sharp or clear cut.
A soft irregular transition is required from time to time.
Develop your experiment but do NOT overwork it.
Gradually modify tones and colours – for example use warm and cool colour to show depth.
Suggest texture by dry-brush or sgraffito techniques - thicker paint may be required to do that.
Do not attempt too much detail - only paint what can be seen by a viewer.
Conclude:
Clean up.

UNIT 1: Experiment 2

Start with the same MMM animal observation as in the previous experiment.

Materials:

Your choice of (dark, light - warm / cool + another colour) non-paint, opaque or transparent paint.

Two brushes (if using paint), white toned or coloured paper (a little larger).

Begin:

Copy one part of the animal from your MMM observation (head, paw, ears).

Use thin paint (large brush) and only show what is necessary.

Then:

Use the dark and light colours to show animal form.

Use thin paint before using thick paint and paint smaller parts later.

Use soft and hard edges for modelling the form.

Boundaries between shapes should not always be too sharp or clear cut.

A soft irregular transition is required from time to time.

Develop your experiment but do NOT overwork it.

Gradually modify tones and colours – for example use warm and cool colour to show depth.

Suggest texture by dry-brush or sgraffito techniques - thicker paint may be required to do that.

Do not attempt too much detail - only paint what can be seen by a viewer.

Conclude:

Clean up.

UNIT 1: Experiment 3

Start with the same MMM animal observation as in the previous experiment.

Materials:

Your choice of (dark, light - warm / cool + another colour) non-paint, opaque or transparent paint.

Two brushes (if using paint), white toned or coloured paper (a little larger).

Begin:

Copy same part of the animal from your MMM observation (head, paw, ears).

Use thin paint (large brush).

Only show what is necessary.

Then:

Use the dark and light colours to show animal form.

Use thin paint before using thick paint.

Paint unimportant areas before important parts.

Paint smaller parts later.

Use soft and hard edges for modelling the form.

Boundaries between shapes should not always be too sharp or clear cut.

A soft irregular transition is required from time to time.

Develop your experiment but do NOT overwork it.

Gradually modify tones and colours – for example use warm and cool colour to show depth.

Suggest texture by dry-brush or sgraffito techniques.

Thicker paint may be required to do that.

Do not attempt too much detail - only paint what can be seen by a viewer.

Conclude:

Clean up.

UNIT 1: Experiment 4

Start with a different MMM animal observation.

Materials:

Your choice of (dark, light - warm / cool + another colour) non-paint, opaque or transparent paint.

Two brushes (if using paint), white toned or coloured paper (a little larger).

Begin:

Copy same part of the animal from your MMM observation (head, paw, ears).

Use thin paint (large brush) and only show what is necessary.

Then:

Use the dark and light colours to show animal form.

Use thin paint before using thick paint.

Paint unimportant areas before important parts.

Paint smaller parts later.

Use soft and hard edges for modelling the form.

Develop your experiment but do NOT overwork it.

Gradually modify tones and colours – for example use warm and cool colour to show depth.

Suggest texture by dry-brush or sgraffito techniques – may require thicker paint.

Do not attempt too much detail - only paint what can be seen by a viewer.

Conclude:

Clean up.

UNIT 1: Experiment 5

Start with a different MMM animal observation.

Materials:

Your choice of (dark, light - warm / cool + another colour) non-paint, opaque or transparent paint.

Two brushes (if using paint), white toned or coloured paper (a little larger).

Begin:

Copy same part of the animal from your MMM observation (head, paw, ears).

Include an extra component (dish, kennel, environment)

Use thin paint (large brush) and only show what is necessary.

Then:

Use the dark and light colours to show animal form.

At the same time establish the light source.

Paint unimportant areas before important parts.

Paint the background to establish brightness of the painting (light/dark).

Use thin paint before using thick paint and paint smaller parts later.

Use soft and hard edges for modelling the form.

Develop your experiment but do NOT overwork it.

Gradually modify tones and colours – for example use warm and cool colour to show depth.

Suggest texture by dry-brush or sgraffito techniques – may require thicker paint.

Do not attempt too much detail - only paint what can be seen by a viewer.

Conclude:

Clean up.

UNIT 1: Experiment 6

Start with a different MMM animal observation.

Materials:

Your choice of (dark, light - warm / cool + another colour) non-paint, opaque or transparent paint.

Two brushes (if using paint), white toned or coloured paper (a little larger).

Begin:

Copy same part of the animal from your MMM observation (head, paw, ears).

Include an extra component (dish, kennel, environment)

Use thin paint (large brush) and only show what is necessary.

Then:

Note the direction of the light.

Use the dark and light colours to show animal form.

Paint unimportant areas before important parts.

Paint the background to establish brightness of the painting (light/dark).

Use thin paint before using thick paint and paint smaller parts later.

Use soft and hard edges for modelling the form.

Develop your experiment but do NOT overwork it.

Gradually modify tones and colours – for example use warm and cool colour to show depth.

Suggest texture by dry-brush or sgraffito techniques – may require thicker paint.

Do not attempt too much detail - only paint what can be seen by a viewer.

Conclude:

Clean up.

Further thoughts:

Use other observations of your own to explore other views.

Suggest animal shape by painting background first.

Paint an animal with as few brushstrokes as possible.

SECOND Experience Unit:

UNIT 2: Experiment 1

Start based on an MMM animal observation you have made.

Materials:

Your choice of (dark, light - warm / cool + another colour) non-paint, opaque or transparent paint.

Two brushes (if using paint), white toned or coloured paper (a little larger).

Begin:

Copy a different part of the animal from your MMM observation (head, paw, ears).

Include an extra component (dish, kennel, environment)

Paint the background to establish brightness of the painting (light/dark).

Use thin paint (large brush) and only show what is necessary.

Then:

Establish a single source for the light.

Use the dark and light colours to show animal form.

Use thin paint before using thick paint.

Paint unimportant areas before important parts.

Paint smaller parts later.

Use soft and hard edges for modelling the form.

Develop your experiment but do NOT overwork it.

Gradually modify tones and colours – for example use warm and cool colour to show depth.

Suggest texture by dry-brush or sgraffito techniques - under-paint before laying on thicker paint.

Conclude:

Clean up.

UNIT 2: Experiment 2

Base start on a different MMM animal observation used in the previous experiment.

Materials:

Your choice of (dark, light - warm / cool + animal colour) non-paint, opaque or transparent paint.

Two brushes (if using paint), white toned or coloured paper (a little larger).

Begin:

Copy same part of the animal from your MMM observation (head, paw, ears).

Use thin paint (large brush) and only show what is necessary.

Include an extra component (dish, kennel, environment)

Paint the background to establish brightness of the painting (light/dark).

Then:

Establish a single source for the light.

Use the dark and light colours to show animal form.

Use thin paint before using thick paint.

Paint unimportant areas before important parts.

Paint smaller parts later.

Use soft and hard edges for modelling the form.

Develop your experiment but do NOT overwork it.

Gradually modify tones and colours – for example use warm and cool colour to show depth.

Suggest texture by dry-brush or sgraffito techniques - under-paint before laying on thicker paint.

Conclude:

Clean up.

UNIT 2: Experiment 3

Base start on a different MMM animal observation used in the previous experiment.

Materials:

Your choice of (dark, light - warm / cool + animal colour) non-paint, opaque or transparent paint.

Two brushes (if using paint), white toned or coloured paper (a little larger).

Begin:

Copy same part of the animal from your MMM observation (head, paw, ears).

Use thin paint (large brush) and only show what is necessary.

Include an extra component (dish, kennel, environment)

Paint the background to establish brightness of the painting (light/dark).

Then:

Establish direction of the light.

Use the dark and light colours to show animal form.

Use thin paint before using thick paint.

Paint unimportant areas before important parts.

Work from most distant to closest areas.

Paint smaller parts later.

Use soft and hard edges for modelling the form.

Develop your experiment but do NOT overwork it.

Gradually modify tones and colours – for example use warm and cool colour to show depth.

Suggest texture by dry-brush or sgraffito techniques and under-paint beforehand.

Conclude:

Clean up.

UNIT 2: Experiment 4

Base start on a different MMM animal observation used in the previous experiment.

Materials:

Your choice of (dark, light - warm / cool + animal colour) non-paint, opaque or transparent paint.

Two brushes (if using paint), white toned or coloured paper (a little larger).

Begin:

Copy same part of the animal from your MMM observation (head, paw, ears).

Use thin paint (large brush) and only show what is necessary.

Include an extra component (dish, kennel, environment)

Paint the background to establish brightness of the painting (light/dark).

Then:

Establish direction of the light then use the dark and light colours to show animal form.

Use thin paint before using thick paint.

Paint unimportant areas before important parts.

Work from most distant to closest areas and paint smaller parts later.

Use soft and hard edges for modelling the form.

Develop your experiment but do NOT overwork it.

Gradually modify tones and colours – for example use warm and cool colour to show depth.

Suggest texture by dry-brush or sgraffito techniques and under-paint beforehand.

Conclude:

Clean up.

UNIT 2: Experiment 5

Base start on a different MMM animal observation used in the previous experiment.

Materials:

Your choice of (dark, light - warm / cool + animal colour) non-paint, opaque or transparent paint.

Two brushes (if using paint), white toned or coloured paper (a little larger).

Begin:

Copy same part of the animal from your MMM observation (head, paw, ears).

Use thin paint (large brush) and only show what is necessary.

Include an extra component (dish, kennel, environment)

Paint the background to establish brightness of the painting (light/dark).

Then:

Establish direction of the light then use the dark and light colours to show animal form.

Use thin paint before using thick paint.

Paint unimportant areas before important parts.

Work from most distant to closest areas.

Paint smaller parts later.

Use soft and hard edges for modelling the form.

Develop your experiment but do NOT overwork it.

Gradually modify tones and colours – using cool before warm to show depth.

Suggest texture by dry-brush or sgraffito techniques and under-paint beforehand.

Conclude:

Clean up.

UNIT 2: Experiment 6

Base start on a different MMM animal observation used in the previous experiment.

Materials:

Your choice of (dark, light - warm / cool + animal colour) non-paint, opaque or transparent paint.

Two brushes (if using paint), white toned or coloured paper (a little larger).

Begin:

Copy same part of the animal from your MMM observation (head, paw, ears).

Use thin paint (large brush) and only show what is necessary.

Include an extra component (dish, kennel, environment)

Paint the background to establish brightness of the painting (light/dark).

Then:

Establish direction of the light then use the dark and light colours to show animal form.

Use thin paint before using thick paint.

Paint unimportant areas before important parts.

Work from most distant to closest areas.

Paint smaller parts later.

Use soft and hard edges for modelling the form.

Develop your experiment but do NOT overwork it.

Gradually modify tones and colours – using cool before warm to show depth.

Suggest texture by dry-brush or sgraffito techniques and under-paint beforehand.

Conclude:

Clean up.

Further thoughts:
Paint animal silhouettes.
Paint background to suggest shape of animal.
Paint an animal with as few brushstrokes as possible.
Use a spotlight to experiment with different sources and directions of lighting.

THIRD Experience Unit:

UNIT 3: Experiment 1
Start based on two different MMM animal observations you have made.
Materials:
Your choice of (dark, light - warm / cool + animal colour) non-paint, opaque or transparent paint.
Two brushes (if using paint), white toned or coloured paper (a little larger).
Begin:
Copy the same part of each animal from your MMM observations (head, paw, ears).
Use thin paint (large brush) and only show what is necessary.
Paint the background to establish brightness of the painting (light/dark).
Then:
Establish direction of the light then use the dark and light colours to show animal form.
Use thin paint before using thick paint.
Paint unimportant areas before important parts.
Use larger brush for larger areas and paint smaller parts later.
Work from most distant to closest areas.
Use soft and hard edges for modelling the form.
Decide the dominant colours.
Develop your experiment but do NOT overwork it.
Gradually modify tones and colours – using cool before warm to show depth.
Suggest texture by dry-brush or sgraffito techniques and under-paint beforehand.
Conclude:

Clean up.

UNIT 3: Experiment 2

Start based on two different MMM animal observations you have made.

Materials:

Your choice of (dark, light - warm / cool + animal colour) non-paint, opaque or transparent paint.

Two brushes (if using paint), white toned or coloured paper (a little larger).

Begin:

Copy the same part of each animal from your MMM observations (head, paw, ears).

Establish direction of the light then use the dark and light colours to show animal form.

Use thin paint (large brush) and only show what is necessary.

Paint unimportant areas before important parts.

Paint the background to establish brightness of the painting (light/dark).

Use larger brush for larger areas and paint smaller parts later.

Use thin paint before using thick paint.

Decide the dominant colours and under-paint accordingly.

Suggest texture by dry-brush or sgraffito techniques and under-paint beforehand.

Then:

Work from most distant to closest areas - use soft and hard edges for modelling the form.

Boundary between shapes isn't always sharp or precise.

Develop your experiment but do NOT overwork it.

Gradually modify tones and colours – using cool before warm to show depth.

Conclude:

Clean up.

UNIT 3: Experiment 3

Start based on two different MMM animal observations you have made.

Materials:

Your choice of (dark, light - warm / cool + animal colour) non-paint, opaque or transparent paint.

Two brushes (if using paint), white toned or coloured paper (a little larger).

Begin:

Copy a different part of the animal from each MMM observation (head, paw, ears).

Copy the same part for each animal.

Note light source.

Paint unimportant areas before important parts.

Use thin paint (large brush) and only show what is necessary.

Use larger brush for larger areas and paint smaller parts later.

Use thin paint before using thick paint.

Decide the dominant colours and under-paint accordingly.

Suggest texture by dry-brush or sgraffito techniques and under-paint beforehand.

Then:

Note direction of the light and keep it consistent through the experiment.

Paint the background to establish brightness of the painting (light/dark).

Paint dark and light areas to show the form of the animal.

Use soft and hard edges for modelling the form.

Work from most distant to closest areas.

Boundary between shapes isn't always sharp or precise.

Develop your experiment but do NOT overwork it.

Gradually modify tones and colours – using cool before warm to show depth.

Conclude:

Clean up.

UNIT 3: Experiment 4

Start based on three different MMM animal observations you have made.

Materials:

Your choice of (dark, light - warm / cool + animal colour) non-paint, opaque or transparent paint.

Two brushes (if using paint), white toned or coloured paper (a little larger).

Begin:

Copy same part of the animal as previously from the MMM observations (head, paw, ears).

Blend the two MMM animal observation memories.

Plan the light source and paint unimportant areas before important parts.

Use thin paint (large brush) and only show what is necessary.

Use larger brush for larger areas and paint smaller parts later - use thin before thick paint.

Decide the dominant colours and under-paint accordingly.

Suggest texture by dry-brush or sgraffito techniques and under-paint beforehand.

Then:

Note direction of the light and keep it consistent through the experiment.

Paint the background to establish brightness of the painting (light/dark).

Paint dark and light areas to show the form of the animal.

Use soft and hard edges for modelling the form - work from most distant to closest areas.

Boundary between shapes isn't always sharp or precise.

Develop your experiment but do NOT overwork it.

Gradually modify tones and colours – using cool before warm to show depth.

Conclude:

Clean up.

UNIT 3: Experiment 5

Start based on another different MMM animal observation you have made.

Materials:

Your choice of (dark, light - warm / cool + animal colour) non-paint, opaque or transparent paint.

Two brushes (if using paint), white toned or coloured paper (a little larger).

Begin:

Copy two different parts of the animal from the MMM observation (head, paw, ears).

Plan the light source and paint unimportant areas before important parts.

Use thin paint (large brush) and only show what is necessary.

Use larger brush for larger areas and paint smaller parts later.

Use thin paint before using thick paint.

Decide the dominant colours and under-paint accordingly.

Suggest texture by dry-brush or sgraffito techniques and under-paint beforehand.

Then:

Note direction of the light and keep it consistent through the experiment.

Paint the background to establish brightness of the painting (light/dark).

Paint dark and light areas to show the form of the animal.

Use soft and hard edges for modelling the form - work from most distant to closest areas.

Boundary between shapes isn't always sharp or precise.

Develop your experiment but do NOT overwork it.

Gradually modify tones and colours – using cool before warm to show depth.

Conclude:

Clean up.

UNIT 3: Experiment 6

Start based on a different MMM animal observation you have made.

Materials:

Your choice of (dark, light - warm / cool + animal colour) non-paint, opaque or transparent paint.

Two brushes (if using paint), white toned or coloured paper (a little larger).

Begin:

Copy two different parts of the animal from the MMM observation (head, paw, ears).

Plan the light source.

Paint unimportant areas before important parts.

Use thin paint (large brush) and only show what is necessary.

Use larger brush for larger areas and paint smaller parts later.

Use thin paint before using thick paint.

Decide the dominant colours and under-paint accordingly.

Suggest texture by dry-brush or sgraffito techniques and under-paint beforehand.

Then:

Note direction of the light and keep it consistent through the experiment.

Paint the background to establish brightness of the painting (light/dark).

Paint dark and light areas to show the form of the animal.

Use soft and hard edges for modelling the form.

Work from most distant to closest areas.

Boundary between shapes isn't always sharp or precise.

Develop your experiment but do NOT overwork t.

Gradually modify tones and colours – using cool before warm to show depth.

Conclude:

Clean up.

Further thoughts:

Paint animals doing different things.

Paint background to suggest shape of animal.

Paint an animal with as few brushstrokes as possible.

Use a spotlight to experiment with different sources and directions of lighting.

Focus on soft and hard edges for modelling the form of an animal.

DEVELOPMENT: Extensions

In the Development extension activities:

Draw on what you have learnt.

You can link what you have learned to your own goals.

DEVELOPMENT: Extension 1

Start with an MMM observation.

Materials:

Use the SAME materials as used in a previous experiment from Unit One.

Use the SAME MMM image as used in a previous experiment Unit One.

Begin:

BUT repeat only one of the experiments.

DEVELOPMENT: Extension 2

Start based on an MMM observation you have made.

Materials:

Use the SAME materials as used in a previous experiment from Unit Two.

Use the SAME MMM image as used in a previous experiment Unit Two.

Begin:

BUT repeat only one of the experiments.

DEVELOPMENT: Extension 3

Start based memory of an MMM observation you have made.

Materials:

Use the SAME materials as used in a previous experiment from Unit Three.

Use the SAMEMMM image as used in a previous experiment Unit Three.

Begin:

BUT repeat only one of the experiments.

OBSERVED ANIMALS 2.

FIRST Experience Unit:

UNIT 1: Experiment 1
Start with a MMM animal observation you have made.
Materials:
Your choice of (dark, light - warm / cool / animal colour) non-paint, opaque or transparent paint.
Two brushes (if using paint), white toned or coloured paper (a little larger).
Begin:
Copy two different parts of the animal from the MMM observation (head, paw, ears).
Plan the light source.
Paint unimportant areas before important parts.
Decide the dominant colours plan under-painting.
Use thin paint (larger brush) before using thick pant.
Only show what is necessary.
Paint smaller parts later.
Suggest texture by dry-brush or sgraffito techniques and under-paint beforehand.
Then:
Keep direction of light consistent through the experiment.
Paint the background to establish brightness of the painting (light/dark).
Paint dark and light areas to show the form of the animal.
Boundary between shapes isn't always sharp or precise.
Use soft and hard edges for modelling the form.
Work from most distant to closest areas.
Develop your experiment but do NOT overwork it.
Gradually modify tones and colours – using cool before warm to show depth.
Conclude:
Clean up.

UNIT 1: Experiment 2

Start with a MMM animal observation you have made.

Materials:

Your choice of (dark, light - warm / cool / animal colour) non-paint, opaque or transparent paint.

Two brushes (if using paint), white toned or coloured paper (a little larger).

Begin:

Copy two different parts of the animal from the MMM observation (head, paw, ears).

Plan the light source.

Paint unimportant areas before important parts.

Decide the dominant colours plan under-painting.

Use thin paint (larger brush) before using thick paint - only show what is necessary.

Paint smaller parts later.

Suggest texture by dry-brush or sgraffito techniques and under-paint beforehand.

Then:

Keep direction of light consistent through the experiment.

Paint the background to establish brightness of the painting (light/dark).

Paint dark and light areas to show the form of the animal.

Boundary between shapes isn't always sharp or precise.

Use soft and hard edges for modelling the form.

Work from most distant to closest areas.

Develop your experiment but do NOT overwork it.

Gradually modify tones and colours – using cool before warm to show depth.

Conclude:

Clean up.

UNIT 1: Experiment 3

Start with a MMM animal observation you have made.

Materials:

Your choice of (dark, light - warm / cool + animal colour) non-paint, opaque or transparent paint.

Two brushes (if using paint), white toned or coloured paper (a little larger).

Begin:

Copy two different parts of the animal from the MMM observation (head, paw, ears).

Plan the light source.

Paint unimportant areas before important parts with thin (larger brush) before thick paint.

Decide the dominant colours and plan the under-painting to only show what is necessary.

Start with larger areas and paint smaller parts later.

Suggest texture by dry-brush or sgraffito techniques and under-paint beforehand.

Then:

Keep direction of light consistent through the experiment.

Paint the background to establish brightness of the painting (light/dark).

Paint dark and light areas to show the form of the animal.

Boundary between shapes isn't always sharp or precise.

Use soft and hard edges for modelling the form.

Work from most distant to closest areas - develop your experiment but do NOT overwork it.

Gradually modify tones and colours – using cool before warm to show depth.

Conclude:

Clean up.

UNIT 1: Experiment 4

Start with a MMM animal observation you have made.

Materials:

Your choice of (dark, light - warm / cool + animal colour) non-paint, opaque or transparent paint.

Two brushes (if using paint), white toned or coloured paper (a little larger).

Begin:

Copy two different parts of the animal from the MMM observation (head, paw, ears).

Plan the light source.

Paint unimportant areas before important parts with thin (larger brush) before thick paint.

Decide the dominant colours.

Plan the under-painting to only show what is necessary.

Start with larger areas and paint smaller parts later.

Suggest texture by dry-brush or sgraffito techniques and under-paint beforehand.

Then:

Keep direction of light consistent through the experiment.

Paint the background to establish brightness of the animal (light/dark).

Work from most distant to closest areas.

Paint dark and light areas to show the form of the animal.

Boundary between shapes isn't always sharp or precise.

Use soft and hard edges for modelling the form.

Develop your experiment but do NOT overwork it.

Gradually modify tones and colours – using cool before warm to show depth.

Conclude:

Clean up.

UNIT 1: Experiment 5

Start with a MMM animal observation you have made.

Materials:

Your choice of (dark, light - warm / cool + animal colour) non-paint, opaque or transparent paint.

Two brushes (if using paint), white toned or coloured paper (a little larger).

Begin:

Copy two different parts of the animal from the MMM observation (head, paw, ears).

Plan the light source and keep direction of light consistent through the experiment.

Paint unimportant areas before important parts with thin (larger brush) before thick paint.

Start with larger areas and paint smaller parts later.

Decide the dominant colours and plan the under-painting to only show what is necessary.

Suggest texture by dry-brush or sgraffito techniques and under-paint beforehand.

Then:

Paint the background to establish brightness of the animal (light/dark).

Work from most distant to closest areas.

Paint dark and light areas to show the form of the animal.

Use soft and hard edges for modelling the form.

Develop your experiment but do NOT overwork it.

Gradually modify tones and colours – using cool before warm to show depth.

Conclude:

Clean up.

UNIT 1: Experiment 6

Start with a MMM animal observation you have made.

Materials:

Your choice of (dark, light - warm / cool + animal colour) non-paint, opaque or transparent paint.

Two brushes (if using paint), white toned or coloured paper (a little larger).

Begin:

Copy three different parts of the animal from the MMM observation (head, paw, ears).

Plan the light source and keep direction of light consistent through the experiment.

Paint unimportant areas before important parts with thin (larger brush) before thick paint.

Start with larger areas and paint smaller parts later.

Decide the dominant colours.

Plan the under-painting to only show what is necessary.

Suggest texture by dry-brush or sgraffito techniques and under-paint beforehand.

Then:

Paint the background to establish brightness of the animal (light/dark).

Work from most distant to closest areas.

Paint dark and light areas to show the form of the animal.

Use soft and hard edges for modelling the form.

Develop your experiment but do NOT overwork it.

Gradually modify tones and colours – using cool before warm to show depth.

Conclude:

Clean up.

Further thoughts:

Use different combinations of parts of the animal from the MMM observation (head, paw, ears).

Try another animal.

SECOND Experience Unit:

UNIT 2: Experiment 1

Start with a MMM animal observation you have made.

Materials:

Your choice of (dark, light - warm / cool + animal colour) non-paint, opaque or transparent paint.

Three brushes (if using paint), white toned or coloured paper (a little larger).

Begin:

Copy three parts of the animal from a MMM observation (head, paw, ears) but not whole animal.

Plan the light source and keep direction of light consistent through the experiment.

Paint unimportant areas before important parts with thin (larger brush) before thick paint.

Start with larger areas and paint smaller parts later.

Decide the dominant colours and plan the under-painting to only show what is necessary.

Suggest texture by dry-brush or sgraffito techniques and under-paint beforehand.

Then:

Paint the background to establish brightness of the animal (light/dark).

Work from most distant to closest areas.

Paint dark and light areas to show the form of the animal.

Use soft and hard edges for modelling the form.

Develop your experiment but do NOT overwork it.

Gradually modify tones and colours – using cool before warm to show depth.

Conclude:

Clean up.

UNIT 2: Experiment 2

Start with a MMM animal observation you have made.

Materials:

Your choice of (dark, light - warm / cool + animal colour) non-paint, opaque or transparent paint.

Three brushes (if using paint), white toned or coloured paper (a little larger).

Begin:

Copy three parts of the animal from a MMM observation (head, paw, ears) but not whole animal.

Plan the light source and keep direction of light consistent through the experiment.

Paint unimportant areas before important parts with thin (larger brush) before thick paint.

Start with larger areas and paint smaller parts later.

Decide the dominant colours and plan the under-painting to only show what is necessary.

Suggest texture by dry-brush or sgraffito techniques and under-paint beforehand.

Then:

Paint the background to establish brightness of the animal (light/dark).

Work from most distant to closest areas.

Paint dark and light areas to show the form of the animal.

Use soft and hard edges for modelling the form.

Develop your experiment but do NOT overwork it.

Gradually modify tones and colours – using cool before warm to show depth.

Conclude:

Clean up.

UNIT 2: Experiment 3

Start with a MMM animal observation you have made.

Materials:

Your choice of (dark, light - warm / cool + animal colour) non-paint, opaque or transparent paint.

Three brushes (if using paint), white toned or coloured paper (a little larger).

Begin:

Copy three parts of the animal from a MMM observation (head, paw, ears) but not whole animal.

Plan the light source and keep direction of light consistent through the experiment.

Paint unimportant areas before important parts with thin (larger brush) before thick paint.

Start with larger areas and paint smaller parts later

Decide the dominant colours and plan the under-painting to only show what is necessary.

Suggest texture by dry-brush or sgraffito techniques and under-paint beforehand.

Then:

Paint the background to establish brightness of the animal (light/dark).

Work from most distant to closest areas.

Paint dark and light areas to show the form of the animal.

Use soft and hard edges for modelling the form.

Develop your experiment but do NOT overwork it.

Gradually modify tones and colours – using cool before warm to show depth.

Conclude:

Clean up.

UNIT 2: Experiment 4

Start with a MMM animal observation you have made.

Materials:

Your choice of (dark, light - warm / cool + animal colour) non-paint, opaque or transparent paint.

Three brushes (if using paint), white toned or coloured paper (a little larger).

Begin:

Copy the animal from a MMM observation (whole animal).

Plan the light source and keep direction of light consistent through the experiment.

Paint unimportant areas before important parts with thin (larger brush) before thick paint.

Start with larger areas and paint smaller parts later.

Decide the dominant colours and plan the under-painting to only show what is necessary.

Suggest texture by dry-brush or sgraffito techniques and under-paint beforehand.

Then:

Paint the background to establish brightness of the animal (light/dark).

Work from most distant to closest areas.

Paint dark and light areas to show the form of the animal.

Use soft and hard edges for modelling the form.

Develop your experiment but do NOT overwork it.

Gradually modify tones and colours – using cool before warm to show depth.

Conclude:

Clean up.

UNIT 2: Experiment 5

Start with a MMM animal observation you have made.

Materials:

Your choice of (dark, light - warm / cool + animal colour) non-paint, opaque or transparent paint.

Three brushes (if using paint), white toned or coloured paper (a little larger).

Begin:

Copy the animal from the MMM observation.

Plan the light source and keep direction of light consistent through the experiment.

Paint unimportant areas before important parts with thin before thick paint.

Large brushes before small brushes.

Start with larger areas and paint smaller parts later.

Decide the dominant colours and plan the under-painting to only show what is necessary.

Suggest texture by dry-brush or sgraffito techniques and under-paint beforehand.

Then:

Paint the background to establish brightness of the animal (light/dark).

Work from most distant to closest areas.

Paint dark and light areas to show the form of the animal.

Use soft and hard edges for modelling the form.

Develop your experiment but do NOT overwork it.

Gradually modify tones and colours – using cool before warm to show depth.

Conclude:

Clean up.

UNIT 2: Experiment 6

Start with a MMM animal observation you have made.

Materials:

Your choice of (dark, light - warm / cool + animal colour) non-paint, opaque or transparent paint.

Three brushes (if using paint), white toned or coloured paper (a little larger).

Begin:

Copy the animal from the MMM observation.

Plan the light source and keep direction of light consistent through the experiment.

Paint unimportant areas before important parts with thin before thick paint.

Large brushes before small brushes.

Start with larger areas and paint smaller parts later.

Decide the dominant colours and plan the under-painting to only show what is necessary.

Suggest texture by dry-brush or sgraffito techniques and under-paint beforehand.

Then:

Paint the background to establish brightness of the animal (light/dark).

Work from most distant to closest areas.

Paint dark and light areas to show the form of the animal.

Use soft and hard edges for modelling the form.

Develop your experiment but do NOT overwork it.

Gradually modify tones and colours – using cool before warm to show depth.

Conclude:

Clean up.

Further thoughts:

Experiment with different viewpoints of the animal (above, front, side).

Try different animals from time to time.

They are a similar combination of different elements.

Look for characteristic arrangements for that animal.

Correct colour can come later.

THIRD Experience Unit:

UNIT 3: Experiment 1

Start with a MMM animal observation you have made.

Materials:

Your choice of (dark, light - warm / cool + animal colour) non-paint, opaque or transparent paint.

Three brushes (if using paint), white toned or coloured paper (a little larger).

Begin:

Copy the animal from the MMM observation.

Plan the light source and keep direction of light consistent through the experiment.

Paint unimportant areas before important parts with thin before thick paint.

Large brushes before small brushes.

Start with larger areas and paint smaller parts later.

Decide the dominant colours and plan the under-painting to only show what is necessary.

Suggest texture by dry-brush or sgraffito techniques and under-paint beforehand.

Then:

Paint the background to establish brightness of the animal (light/dark).

Work from most distant to closest areas.

Paint dark and light areas to show the form of the animal.

Use soft and hard edges for modelling the form.

Develop your experiment but do NOT overwork it.

Gradually modify tones and colours – using cool before warm to show depth.

Conclude:

Clean up.

UNIT 3: Experiment 2

Start with a different MMM animal observation you have made.

Materials:

Your choice of (dark, light - warm / cool + animal colour) non-paint, opaque or transparent paint.

Three brushes (if using paint), white toned or coloured paper (a little larger).

Begin:

Copy the animal from the MMM observation.

Plan the light source and keep direction of light consistent through the experiment.

Paint unimportant areas before important parts with thin before thick paint.

Large brushes before small brushes.

Start with larger areas and paint smaller parts later.

Decide the dominant colours and plan the under-painting to only show what is necessary.

Suggest texture by dry-brush or sgraffito techniques and under-paint beforehand.

Then:

Paint the background to establish brightness of the animal (light/dark).

Work from most distant to closest areas.

Paint dark and light areas to show the form of the animal.

Use soft and hard edges for modelling the form.

Develop your experiment but do NOT overwork it.

Gradually modify tones and colours – using cool before warm to show depth.

Conclude:

Clean up.

UNIT 3: Experiment 3

Start with another MMM animal observation you have made.

Materials:

Your choice of (dark, light - warm / cool + animal colour) non-paint, opaque or transparent paint.

Three brushes (if using paint), white toned or coloured paper (a little larger).

Begin:

Copy the animal from the MMM observation.

Plan the light source and keep direction of light consistent through the experiment.

Paint unimportant areas before important parts with thin before thick paint.

Large brushes before small brushes.

Start with larger areas and paint smaller parts later.

Decide the dominant colours and plan the under-painting to only show what is necessary.

Suggest texture by dry-brush or sgraffito techniques and under-paint beforehand.

Then:

Paint the background to establish brightness of the animal (light/dark).

Work from most distant to closest areas.

Paint dark and light areas to show the form of the animal.

Use soft and hard edges for modelling the form.

Develop your experiment but do NOT overwork it.

Gradually modify tones and colours – using cool before warm to show depth.

Conclude:

Clean up.

UNIT 3: Experiment 4

Start with two MMM animal observations you have made.

Materials:

Your choice of (dark, light - warm / cool + animal colour) non-paint, opaque or transparent paint.

Three brushes (if using paint), white toned or coloured paper (a little larger).

Begin:

Combine the animals from the MMM observation in your experiment.

Plan the light source and keep direction of light consistent through the experiment.

Paint unimportant areas before important parts with thin before thick paint.

Large brushes before small brushes.

Start with larger areas and paint smaller parts later.

Decide the dominant colours and plan the under-painting to only show what is necessary.

Suggest texture by dry-brush or sgraffito techniques and under-paint beforehand.

Then:

Paint the background to establish brightness of the animal (light/dark).

Work from most distant to closest areas.

Paint dark and light areas to show the form of the animal.

Use soft and hard edges for modelling the form.

Develop your experiment but do NOT overwork it.

Gradually modify tones and colours – using cool before warm to show depth.

Conclude:

Clean up.

UNIT 3: Experiment 5

Start with two MMM animal observations you have made.

Materials:

Your choice of (dark, light - warm / cool + animal colour) non-paint, opaque or transparent paint.

Three brushes (if using paint), white toned or coloured paper (a little larger).

Begin:

Combine the animals from the MMM observation n your experiment.

Plan the light source and keep direction of light consistent through the experiment.

Paint unimportant areas before important parts with thin before thick paint.

Large brushes before small brushes.

Start with larger areas and paint smaller parts later.

Decide the dominant colours and plan the under-painting to only show what is necessary.

Suggest texture by dry-brush or sgraffito techniques and under-paint beforehand.

Then:

Paint the background to establish brightness of the animal (light/dark).

Work from most distant to closest areas.

Paint dark and light areas to show the form of the animal.

Use soft and hard edges for modelling the form.

Develop your experiment but do NOT overwork it.

Gradually modify tones and colours – using cool before warm to show depth.

Conclude:

Clean up.

UNIT3: Experiment 6

Start with several MMM animal observations you have made.

Materials:

Your choice of (dark, light - warm / cool + animal colour) non-paint, opaque or transparent paint.

Three brushes (if using paint), white toned or coloured paper (a little larger).

Begin:

Combine the animals from the MMM observation as a group in your experiment.

Plan the light source and keep direction of light consistent through the experiment.

Paint unimportant areas before important parts with thin before thick paint.

Large brushes before small brushes.

Start with larger areas and paint smaller parts later.

Decide the dominant colours and plan the under-painting to only show what is necessary.

Suggest texture by dry-brush or sgraffito techniques and under-paint beforehand.

Then:

Paint the background to establish brightness of the animal (light/dark).

Work from most distant to closest areas.

Paint dark and light areas to show the form of the animal.

Use soft and hard edges for modelling the form.

Develop your experiment but do NOT overwork it.

Gradually modify tones and colours – using cool before warm to show depth.

Conclude:

Clean up.

Further thoughts:
Experiment with different groups of the animal.
Also experiment with different viewpoints (top, side, rear, front) of the animal.
Try different animals from time to time.
They are a similar combination of different elements.
Look for characteristic arrangements for that animal.
Correct colour can come later.
Make a study box.
Cut down a box so it is like a small room with a floor and two or even three sides.
Toy animals can be placed in the study box.
The floor and walls can be painted differently from time to time.

DEVELOPMENT: Extensions

In the Development extension activities:

Draw on what you have learnt.

You can link what you have learned to your own goals.

DEVELOPMENT: Extension 1

Start with an MMM observation.

Materials:

Use the SAME materials as used in a previous experiment from Unit One.

Use the SAME MMM image as used in a previous experiment Unit One.

Begin:

BUT repeat only one of the experiments.

DEVELOPMENT: Extension 2

Start based on an MMM observation you have made.

Materials:

Use the SAME materials as used in a previous experiment from Unit Two.

Use the SAME MMM image as used in a previous experiment Unit Two.

Begin:

BUT repeat only one of the experiments.

DEVELOPMENT: Extension 3

Start based memory of an MMM observation you have made.

Materials:

Use the SAME materials as used in a previous experiment from Unit Three.

Use the SAME MMM image as used in a previous experiment Unit Three.

Begin:

BUT repeat only one of the experiments.

CONGRATULATIONS.

You have taken the OBSERVATION pathway.

This could be the final step to being the artist you want to be.

The third pathway is linked to your IMAGINATION.

IMAGINARY ANIMALS.

Limited material encourages more thoughtful responses.
Creativity, an ability to do most with least, is developed.
In art as in science the task of combining many variables is highly skilled.
Repeat something rather than use too great a variety of materials.

The artist, during the act of creating a work is expressing something.
Expression is a unique personal action.

Three artists attempt to paint the same subject, exactly as seen.
They will finish with three different works.
The differences can be attributed to the various artists' expression.
Their works are symbols for this expression.

Expression is related to emotion.
Although the individual may not be conscious of what that emotion is.
The presence of emotion creates a tension (a feeling).
The tension isn't necessarily emotion, but an awareness of an emotional state.

Expression brings into perceptual form symbols for that awareness.
It is thus related to that the underlying emotional state.

The expressive act is not necessarily related to any particular audience.
There's a difference in arousing emotion in an audience, which is intended.
This is manipulative and a form of communication.

A similar arousal can be the result of expression.
Such expression denotes and belongs to an individual.
It is actually a characteristic of individuals.
It's not communication but observers are often mistaken in this regard.

Expressing and exhibiting symptoms of emotion are different.
The first is necessary for artistic activity and a personal reaction to a stimulus.

Symptoms of emotion are what an observer sees.
They may be manipulation of symbols without any emotion at all (actor).

The relationship between an artist and the work is thus a personal one.
It's linked to the inner state of an artist prior to, and during creating.
That may ultimately result in a work of art.

It doesn't really matter what you do at the start.
The most important thing is to actually do something.
Let's see what happens here when I do this?

Random starts do not necessarily have to be the case.
You can plan your starts BUT take your time.
Don't rush just enjoy the experience and see what you can find out.

Once you begin, you can alter or change what you have done.
It's better to do something and be wrong, than do nothing.
Mistakes can be corrected, and you learn what not to do at the same time.
Any MMM experiment does not even have to be finished!

In the process you'll discover whatever you find out.
More importantly the discoveries are yours.
They're part of actual experience rather than just part of following instructions.

Your knowledge grows from your own experiences.
This is what real learning is about.
Your experience and confidence grows for the more you do the better you get!

You are the judge of quality, which is a variable that changes over time.
You probably have old works you thought were excellent at the time done.
What are they like now?

Continue with the subject matter you want to paint really well.
That way you are continuing down the correct path (for you).

Your focus is always on animals.

But now you are imagining your chosen painting focus.

This means you are NOT limited to things you can actually look at.

Make notes, do sketches and record your thoughts.

This is material you can draw on when continuing your MMM experiments.

Carry a small sketchpad or even scraps of paper and a pen or pencil.

Your observation helps you understand animals.

Over time you will develop the individual paining skills needed.

You will also know how to paint your subject your way.

That means you can take liberties in regard to what you see.

Eventually you can focus on another subject.

If it is related to your original theme you will learn much quicker.

From one breed of dog to another is an example.

Then from one kind of animal to another.

Totally imaginary animals are an extension of this process.

You'll note the similarities and also the differences.

Follow this pattern long enough, and you'll be able to paint anything you want!

People who do things well also do them faster than those who don't.

That applies to painting just as much as anything else.

It's one of the indicators of skill.

By now you should have noticed that repetition helps skill development.

Several small paintings are better for learning than one larger one (more time).

That's how you can apply what you have learnt.

Skill in art, sport or even medicine is basically the same phenomenon.

It's practiced behaviour in action.

Most artists don't do anywhere near enough paintings to develop any real skill.

Work on several experiments at the same time increases productivity.
For you reduce wasted time.
Run into a dead-end with one painting move to another for a fresh start.
When the painting is returned to, there will be a different attitude.
Otherwise set it aside again.

Working on a number of experiments at the same time saves materials.
A particular colour can be applied to the work for which it was intended.
BUT there will other works where that same colour will be appropriate.
When you buy paint, buy in quantity, but only use as needed.

Avoid major works.
They take time (years), usually done slowly and are often large and complex.
You'll tend to labour over them as you seek to do your best.
You might occasionally do a slightly larger experiment.

Focus on learning what you can.
Action with materials = technique.
Practiced techniques = skill.
Habitual technique + skill = style.

Do you have an ideas book?
You are probably familiar with a sketchbook.
An Ideas Book is any book just where you write, scribble, draw, or make notes.
It doesn't really matter whether it has lines or the pages are blank.

It will be full of your ideas, or memory aids for your ideas in most cases.
Naturally ideas for paintings will be there.
Writing down thoughts is a way to commit them to your memory bank.
Then they are accessible later.
Look at pages in your Ideas Book at a later date will refresh those ideas.
That will go beyond what is merely recorded in your book.

Writing ideas down builds a bridge between what you think and actions to take.

Do you plan effectively?
Your Ideas Book can be where you start your planning.
Sometimes this will be repetitive, as minor variations are tested.
But they have to be worked through to find out what happens.
Effective planning is the beginnings of effective actions.
Your plans are the test runs for the real world.
Plans don't make anything happen, but they certainly ease the way.
Your preparation can be quite systematic!

How will you get the most from your Ideas Book?
You'll always get more from what you draw or write rather than read or hear.
Carry out sensible ideas with a chance that you'll improve on your past efforts.
If you do not try anything then there is no chance of an improvement at all.

This is particularly useful when you are observing fleeting thoughts.
Sometimes they'll turn out great, but at other times not so.
But you don't need to be brave for there is no risk.

NOW START: IMAGINARY ANIMALS

FIRST Experience Unit:

UNIT 1: Experiment 1

Imagine a distorted MMM image to start.

Materials:

Your choice of (dark, light - warm / cool + dominant colour) non-paint, opaque or transparent paint.

Three brushes (if using paint), white toned or coloured paper (a little larger).

Preparation:

Distort the animal from the MMM image in your experiment.

Add another image (not animal) into the experiment.

Decide the dominant colour.

Consider the tonal arrangement.

Think about the spaces

Begin:

Large brushes before small brushes.

Start with larger areas and paint smaller parts later – basic construction.

Paint unimportant areas before important parts but only what is essential.

Thin before thick paint.

Then:

Paint the background to establish brightness of the animal (light/dark).

Under-paint with the dominant colour.

Paint dark and light areas to show the form of the animal.

Now:

Gradually modify tones and colours – using cool before warm to show depth.

Use tone to show depth (perspective) – light to dark.

Lightest tone most distant.

Continue:

Use soft and hard edges for modelling the form.

Suggest texture by dry-brush or sgraffito techniques, under-paint beforehand.

Develop your experiment but do NOT overwork it.

Conclude: Clean up.

UNIT 1: Experiment 2

Imagine a distorted MMM image to start.

Materials:

Choice of (dark, light - warm / cool + dominant colour) non-paint, opaque or transparent paint.

Three brushes (if using paint), white toned or coloured paper (a little larger).

Preparation:

Distort the animal from the MMM image in your experiment.

Add another image (not animal) into the experiment.

Decide the dominant colour.

Consider the tonal arrangement.

Think about the spaces

Begin:

Start with larger areas and paint smaller parts later – basic construction.

Paint unimportant areas before important parts.

But only what is essential.

Then:

Paint the background to establish brightness of the animal (light/dark).

Under-paint with the dominant colour.

Paint dark and light areas to show the form of the animal.

Thin before thick paint.

Cool colour before warm.

Now:

Gradually modify tones and colours – using cool before warm to show depth.

Use tone to show depth (perspective) – darkest tone most distant.

Continue:

Use soft and hard edges for modelling the form.

Suggest texture by dry-brush or sgraffito techniques and under-paint beforehand.

Develop your experiment but do NOT overwork it.

Conclude:

Clean up.

UNIT 1: Experiment 3

Imagine a distorted MMM image to start.

Materials:

Choice of (dark, light - warm / cool + dominant colour) non-paint, opaque or transparent paint.

Three brushes (if using paint), white toned or coloured paper (a little larger).

Preparation:

Distort the animal from the MMM image in your experiment.

Add another image (not animal) into the experiment.

Decide the dominant colour.

Consider the tonal arrangement.

Think about the spaces

Begin:

Start with larger areas and paint smaller parts later – basic construction.

Paint unimportant areas before important parts.

But only what is essential.

Then:

Paint the background to establish brightness of the animal (light/dark).

Under-paint with the dominant colour.

Paint dark and light areas to show the form of the animal.

Thin before thick paint.

Cool colour before warm.

Now:

Gradually modify tones and colours – using cool before warm to show depth.

Use tone to show depth (perspective) – darkest tone most distant.

Continue:

Use soft and hard edges for modelling the form.

Suggest texture by dry-brush or sgraffito techniques and under-paint beforehand.

Develop your experiment but do NOT overwork it.

Conclude:

Clean up.

UNIT 1: Experiment 4

Imagine a distorted MMM image to start.

Materials:

Choice of (dark, light - warm / cool + dominant colour) non-paint, opaque or transparent paint.

Three brushes (if using paint), white toned or coloured paper (a little larger).

Preparation:

Distort the animal from the MMM image in your experiment.

Add two other images (not animal) into the experiment.

Decide the dominant colour.

Consider the tonal arrangement.

Think about the spaces

Begin:

Start with larger areas and paint smaller parts later – basic construction.

Paint unimportant areas before important parts.

But only what is essential.

Then:

Paint the background to establish brightness of the animal (light/dark).

Under-paint with the dominant colour.

Paint dark and light areas to show the form of the animal.

Thin before thick paint.

Cool colour before warm.

Now:

Gradually modify tones and colours – using cool before warm to show depth.

Use tone to show depth (perspective) – darkest tone most distant.

Continue:

Use soft and hard edges for modelling the form.

Suggest texture by dry-brush or sgraffito techniques and under-paint beforehand.

Develop your experiment but do NOT overwork it.

Conclude:

Clean up.

UNIT 1: Experiment 5

Imagine a distorted MMM image to start.

Materials:

Choice of (dark, light - warm / cool + dominant colour) non-paint, opaque or transparent paint.

Three brushes (if using paint), white toned or coloured paper (a little larger).

Preparation:

Distort the animal from the MMM image in your experiment.

Add two other images (not animal) into the experiment.

Decide the dominant colour.

Consider the tonal arrangement.

Think about the spaces

Begin:

Start with larger areas and paint smaller parts later – basic construction.

Paint unimportant areas before important parts.

But only what is essential.

Then:

Paint the background to establish brightness of the animal (light/dark).

Under-paint with the dominant colour.

Paint dark and light areas to show the form of the animal.

Thin before thick paint.

Cool colour before warm.

Now:

Gradually modify tones and colours – using cool before warm to show depth.

Use tone to show depth (perspective) – darkest tone most distant.

Continue:

Use soft and hard edges for modelling the form.

Suggest texture by dry-brush or sgraffito techniques and under-paint beforehand.

Develop your experiment but do NOT overwork it.

Conclude:

Clean up.

UNIT 1: Experiment 6

Imagine a distorted MMM image to start.

Materials:

Choice of (dark, light - warm / cool + dominant colour) non-paint, opaque or transparent paint.

Three brushes (if using paint), white toned or coloured paper (a little larger).

Preparation:

Distort the animal from the MMM image in your experiment.

Add two other images (not animal) into the experiment.

Decide the dominant colour.

Consider the tonal arrangement.

Think about the spaces

Begin:

Start with larger areas and paint smaller parts later – basic construction.

Paint unimportant areas before important parts.

But only what is essential.

Then:

Focus experiment on colour.

Paint the background to establish brightness of the animal (light/dark).

Under-paint with the dominant colour.

Paint dark and light areas to show the form of the animal.

Thin before thick paint.

Cool colour before warm.

Now:

Gradually modify tones and colours – using cool before warm to show depth.

Use tone to show depth (perspective) – darkest tone most distant.

Continue:

Use soft and hard edges for modelling the form.

Suggest texture by dry-brush or sgraffito techniques and under-paint beforehand.

Develop your experiment but do NOT overwork it

Conclude:

Clean up.

Further thoughts:

Experiment with the focus on different elements (colour, tone, shape, line, etc).

Also experiment with different principles (harmony, contrast, etc).

Also vary the viewpoint of your imaginary animal.

SECOND Experience Unit:

UNIT 2: Experiment 1

Imagine a semi-abstract MMM image to start.

Consider the visual element: Space

The factor that indicates emptiness or a break.

Space relates to the lack of obvious other element (particularly mass and line).

However space usually relates to being inside, outside, under or over.

Space may be open (incomplete) or closed (has a boundary).

Space also may be actual or implied.

It is sometimes termed environment.

Materials:

Choice of (dark, light - warm / cool + dominant colour) non-paint, opaque or transparent paint.

Three brushes (if using paint), white toned or coloured paper (a little larger).

Preparation:

Distort the animal from the MMM image in your experiment.

Add two or more other images (not animal) into the experiment.

Decide the dominant colour.

Consider the tonal arrangement.

Think about the spaces

Begin:

Start with larger areas and paint smaller parts later – basic construction.

Paint unimportant areas before important parts.

But only what is essential.

Then:

Focus experiment on colour.

Paint the background to establish brightness of the animal (light/dark).

Under-paint with the dominant colour.

Paint dark and light areas to show the form of the animal.

Thin before thick paint.

Cool colour before warm.

Now:

Gradually modify tones and colours – using cool before warm to show depth.

Use tone to show depth (perspective) – lightest tone most distant.

Continue:

Use soft and hard edges for modelling the form.

Suggest texture by dry-brush or sgraffito techniques and under-paint beforehand.

Develop your experiment but do NOT overwork it

Conclude:

Clean up.

UNIT 2: Experiment 2

Imagine a semi-abstract MMM image to start.

Consider the visual element: Space

The factor that indicates emptiness or a break.

Space relates to the lack of obvious other element (particularly mass and line).

However space usually relates to being inside, outside, under or over.

Space may be open (incomplete) or closed (has a boundary).

Space also may be actual or implied.

Materials:

Choice of (dark, light - warm / cool + dominant colour) non-paint, opaque or transparent paint.

Three brushes (if using paint), white toned or coloured paper (a little larger).

Preparation:

Distort the animal from the MMM image in your experiment.

Add two or more other images (not animal) into the experiment.

Decide the dominant colour.

Consider the tonal arrangement.

Think about the spaces

Begin:

Start with larger areas and paint smaller parts later – basic construction.

Paint unimportant areas before important parts.

But only what is essential.

Then:

Focus experiment on colour.

Paint the background to establish brightness of the animal (light/dark).

Under-paint with the dominant colour.

Paint dark and light areas to show the form of the animal.

Thin before thick paint.

Cool colour before warm.

Now:

Gradually modify tones and colours – using cool before warm to show depth.

Use tone to show depth (perspective) – darkest tone most distant.

Continue:

Use soft and hard edges for modelling the form.

Suggest texture by dry-brush or sgraffito techniques and under-paint beforehand.

Develop your experiment but do NOT overwork it.

Conclude:

Clean up.

UNIT 2: Experiment 3

Imagine a semi-abstract MMM image to start.

Consider the visual element: Space

The factor that indicates emptiness or a break.

However space usually relates to being inside, outside, under or over.

Space may be open (incomplete) or closed (has a boundary).

Space also may be actual or implied.

Materials:

Choice of (dark, light - warm / cool + dominant colour) non-paint, opaque or transparent paint.

Three brushes (if using paint), white toned or coloured paper (a little larger).

Preparation:

Distort the animal from the MMM image in your experiment.

Add two or more other distorted images (not animal) into the experiment.

Decide the dominant colour.

Consider the tonal arrangement.

Think about the spaces

Begin:

Start with larger areas and paint smaller parts later – basic construction.

Paint unimportant areas before important parts.

But only what is essential.

Then:

Focus experiment on colour.

Paint the background to establish brightness of the animal (light/dark).

Under-paint with the dominant colour.

Paint dark and light areas to show the form of the animal.

Thin before thick paint.

Cool colour before warm.

Now:

Gradually modify tones and colours – using cool before warm to show depth.

Use tone to show depth (perspective) – lightest and darkest tone closest with grey most distant.

Continue:

Use soft and hard edges for modelling the form.

Suggest texture by dry-brush or sgraffito techniques and under-paint beforehand.

Develop your experiment but do NOT overwork it.

Conclude:

Clean up.

UNIT 2: Experiment 4

Imagine a semi-abstract MMM image to start.

Consider the visual element: Space

Space usually relates to being inside, outside, under or over.

Space may be open (incomplete) or closed (has a boundary).

Space also may be actual or implied.

Materials:

Choice of (dark, light - warm / cool + dominant colour) non-paint, opaque or transparent paint.

Three brushes (if using paint), white toned or coloured paper (a little larger).

Preparation:

Distort the animal from the MMM image in your experiment.

Add two or more other distorted images (not animal) into the experiment.

Decide the dominant colour.

Consider the tonal arrangement.

Think about the spaces

Begin:

Start with larger areas and paint smaller parts later – basic construction.

Paint unimportant areas before important parts.

But only what is essential.

Then:

Focus experiment on colour.

Paint the background to establish brightness of the animal (light/dark).

Under-paint with the dominant colour.

Paint dark and light areas to show the form of the animal.

Thin before thick paint.

Cool colour before warm.

Now:

Gradually modify tones and colours – using cool before warm to show depth.

Use tone to show depth (perspective) – lightest ard darkest tone closest with grey most distant.

Continue:

Use soft and hard edges for modelling the form.

Suggest texture by dry-brush or sgraffito techniques and under-paint beforehand.

Develop your experiment but do NOT overwork it.

Conclude:

Clean up.

UNIT 2: Experiment 5

Imagine a semi-abstract MMM image to start.

Consider the visual element: Space

Space may be open (incomplete) or closed (has a boundary).

Space also may be actual or implied.

Materials:

Choice of (dark, light - warm / cool + dominant colour) non-paint, opaque or transparent paint.

Three brushes (if using paint), white toned or coloured paper (a little larger).

Preparation:

Distort the animal from the MMM image in your experiment.

Add two or more other overlapping and distorted images (not animal) into the experiment.

Decide the dominant colour.

Consider the tonal arrangement.

Think about the spaces

Begin:

Start with larger areas and paint smaller parts later – basic construction.

Paint unimportant areas before important parts.

But only what is essential.

Then:

Focus experiment on colour.

Paint the background to establish brightness of the animal (light/dark).

Under-paint with the dominant colour.

Paint dark and light areas to show the form of the animal.

Thin before thick paint.

Cool colour before warm.

Now:

Gradually modify tones and colours – using cool before warm to show depth.

Use tone to show depth (perspective) – lightest and darkest tone closest with grey most distant.

Continue:

Use soft and hard edges for modelling the form.

Suggest texture by dry-brush or sgraffito techniques and under-paint beforehand.

Develop your experiment but do NOT overwork it

Conclude:

Clean up.

UNIT 2: Experiment 6

Imagine a semi-abstract MMM image to start.

Consider the visual element: Space

Space may be open (incomplete) or closed (has a boundary).

Materials:

Choice of (dark, light - warm / cool + dominant colour) non-paint, opaque or transparent paint.

Three brushes (if using paint), white toned or coloured paper (a little larger).

Preparation:

Distort the animal from the MMM image in your experiment.

Add two or more overlapping and distorted images (not animal) into the experiment.

Decide the dominant colour.

Consider the tonal arrangement.

Think about the spaces

Begin:

Start with larger areas and paint smaller parts later – basic construction.

Paint unimportant areas before important parts.

But only what is essential.

Then:

Focus experiment on colour.

Paint the background to establish brightness of the animal (light/dark).

Under-paint with the dominant colour.

Paint dark and light areas to show the form of the animal.

Thin before thick paint.

Cool colour before warm.

Now:

Gradually modify tones and colours – using cool before warm to show depth.

Use tone to show depth (perspective) – lightest and darkest tone closest with grey most distant.

Continue:

Refocus on the dominant colour and modify local colour accordingly.

Use soft and hard edges for modelling the form.

Suggest texture by dry-brush or sgraffito techniques and under-paint beforehand.

Develop your experiment but do NOT overwork it.

Conclude:

Clean up.

Further thoughts:

Also experiment with different principles (harmony, contrast, etc).

Also vary the viewpoint of your imaginary animal.

Animals have their own colour (local colour).

This could be any colour if you paint consistently.

THIRD Experience Unit:

UNIT 3: Experiment 1

Imagine two semi-abstracted MMM images to start.

Consider the visual element: Direction

The factor that indicates aim or course of movement.

The movement may be real or suggested.

Direction relates to a plane or axis, which may be horizontal, vertical or oblique.

There is a start and an end and can be seen in a serial order or sequence.

There is a link with rhythm and balance.

Materials:

Choice non-paint, opaque or transparent paint

(dark, light, dominant, complementary) colours.

Three brushes (if using paint), white toned or coloured paper (a little larger).

Preparation:

Distort the animals from the MMM images in your experiment.

Add two or more overlapping and distorted images (not animal) into the experiment.

Decide the dominant colour.

Consider the tonal arrangement.

Think about the spaces

Begin:

Start with larger areas and paint smaller parts later – basic construction.

Paint unimportant areas before important parts.

But only what is essential.

Then:

Under-paint with the dominant colour.

Thin before thick paint.

Cool colour before warm.

Now:

Gradually modify tones and colours.

Use tone to show depth (perspective) – lightest and darkest tone closest with grey most distant.

Continue:

Refocus on the dominant colour and modify local colour accordingly.

Use the complementary (opposite) colours in short brushstrokes next to one another.

Use soft and hard edges for modelling.

Suggest texture by dry-brush or sgraffito techniques and under-paint beforehand.

Develop your experiment but do NOT overwork it.

Conclude:

UNIT 3: Experiment 2

Imagine two semi-abstracted MMM images to start.

Consider the visual element: Direction

The factor that indicates aim or course of movement.

The movement may be real or suggested.

Direction relates to a plane or axis, which may be horizontal, vertical or oblique.

There is a start and an end and can be seen in a serial order or sequence.

Materials:

Choice non-paint, opaque or transparent paint (dark, light, dominant, complementary) colours.

Three brushes (if using paint), white toned or coloured paper (a little larger).

Preparation:

Distort the animals from the MMM images in your experiment.

Add two or more overlapping and distorted images (not animal) into the experiment.

Decide the dominant colour.

Consider the tonal arrangement.

Think about the spaces

Begin:

Start with larger areas and paint smaller parts later – basic construction.

Paint unimportant areas before important parts.

But only what is essential.

Then:

Under-paint with the dominant colour.

Thin before thick paint.

Cool colour before warm.

Now:

Gradually modify tones and colours.

Use tone to show depth (perspective) – lightest and darkest tone closest with grey most distant.

Continue:

Refocus on the dominant colour and modify local colour accordingly.

Scumble the complementary (opposite) colours in light brushstrokes one on top of the other.

Use soft and hard edges for modelling.

Suggest texture by dry-brush or sgraffito techniques and under-paint beforehand.

Develop your experiment but do NOT overwork it.

Conclude:

Clean up.

UNIT 3: Experiment 3

Imagine two semi-abstracted MMM images to start.

Consider the visual element: Direction

The factor that indicates aim or course of movement.

Direction relates to a plane or axis, which may be horizontal, vertical or oblique.

There is a start and an end and can be seen in a serial order or sequence.

Materials:

Choice non-paint, opaque or transparent paint

(dark, light, dominant, complementary) colours.

Three brushes (if using paint), white toned or coloured paper (a little larger).

Preparation:

Distort the animals from the MMM images in your experiment.

Add two or more overlapping and distorted images (not animal) into the experiment.

Decide the dominant colour.

Consider the tonal arrangement.

Think about the spaces

Begin:

Concentrate on the basic construction of your experiment.

Paint unimportant areas before important parts.

But only what is essential.

Then:

Under-paint with the dominant colour.

Thin before thick paint.

Cool colour before warm.

Now:

Gradually modify tones and colours.

Use tone to show depth (perspective) – lightest and darkest tone closest with grey most distant.

Continue:

Refocus on the dominant colour and modify local colour accordingly.

Use a pointillist technique - complementary (opposite) colours in small dots next to each other.

Use soft and hard edges for modelling.

Suggest texture by dry-brush or sgraffito techniques and under-paint beforehand.

Develop your experiment but do NOT overwork it.

Conclude:

Clean up.

UNIT 3: Experiment 4

Imagine two semi-abstracted MMM images to start.

Consider the visual element: Direction

The factor that indicates aim or course of movement.

Direction relates to a plane or axis, which may be horizontal, vertical or oblique.

Materials:

Choice dark, light, dominant, complementary colours (two harmonious one complementary).

Three brushes (if using paint), white toned or coloured paper (a little larger).

Preparation:

Distort the animals from the MMM images in your experiment.

Add two or more overlapping and distorted images (not animal) into the experiment.

Imagine some reflections of the semi-abstract animal images.

Decide the colour scheme (two harmonious one complementary).

Consider the tonal arrangement.

Think about the spaces

Begin:

Concentrate on the basic construction of your experiment.

Paint unimportant areas before important parts.

But only what is essential.

Then:

Under-paint with the dominant colour.

Thin before thick paint.

Cool colour before warm.

Now:

Gradually modify tones and colours.

Use tone to show depth (perspective) – lightest and darkest tone closest with grey most distant.

Reflections are upside down images.

If the surface is disturbed (water) reflections are darker.

A shiny or glossy surface takes some of the reflected local colour.

Continue:

Refocus on the dominant colour and modify local colour accordingly.

Use a pointillist technique - complementary (opposite) colours in small dots next to each other.

Use soft and hard edges for modelling.

Suggest texture by dry-brush or sgraffito techniques and under-paint beforehand.

Develop your experiment but do NOT overwork it.

Conclude:

Clean up.

UNIT 3: Experiment 5

Imagine two semi-abstracted MMM images to start.

Consider the visual element: Direction

The factor that indicates aim or course of movement.

Materials:

Choice dark, light, dominant, complementary colours (two harmonious one complementary).

The colours should be different from those used in the last experiment.

Three brushes (if using paint), white toned or coloured paper (a little larger).

Preparation:

Distort the animals from the MMM images in your experiment.

Add two or more overlapping and distorted images (not animal) into the experiment.

Imagine some reflections of the semi-abstract animal images.

Decide the colour scheme (two harmonious one complementary) but different from previously.

Consider the tonal arrangement.

Think about the spaces

Begin:

Concentrate on the basic construction of your experiment.

Paint unimportant areas before important parts.

But only what is essential.

Then:

Under-paint with the dominant colour.

Thin before thick paint.

Cool colour before warm.

Now:

Gradually modify tones and colours.

Use tone to show depth (perspective) – lightest and darkest tone closest with grey most distant.

Reflections are upside down images.

If the surface is disturbed (water) reflections are darker.

A shiny or glossy surface takes some of the reflected local colour.

Continue:

Refocus on the dominant colour and modify local colour accordingly.

Use a pointillist technique - complementary (opposite) colours in small dots next to each other.

Use soft and hard edges for modelling.

Suggest texture by dry-brush or sgraffito techniques and under-paint beforehand.

Develop your experiment but do NOT overwork it.

Conclude:

Clean up.

UNIT 3: Experiment 6

Imagine two semi-abstracted MMM images to start.

Consider the visual element: Direction

The factor that indicates aim or course of movement.

Materials:

Choice dark, light, dominant, complementary colours (two harmonious one complementary).

The colours should be different from those used in the last experiment.

Three brushes (if using paint), white toned or coloured paper (a little larger).

Preparation:

Distort the animals from the MMM images in your experiment.

Add two or more overlapping and distorted images (not animal) into the experiment.

Imagine some reflections of the semi-abstract animal images.

Decide the colour scheme (two harmonious one complementary) but different from previously.

Consider the tonal arrangement.

Think about the spaces

Begin:

Concentrate on the basic construction of your experiment.

Paint unimportant areas before important parts.

But only what is essential.

Then:

Under-paint with the dominant colour.

Thin before thick paint.

Cool colour before warm.

Now:

Gradually modify tones and colours.

Use tone to show depth (perspective) – lightest and darkest tone closest with grey most distant.

Reflections are upside down images.

If the surface is disturbed (water) reflections are darker.

A shiny or glossy surface takes some of the reflected local colour.

Continue:

Refocus on the dominant colour and modify local colour accordingly.

Use a pointillist technique - complementary (opocsite) colours in small dots next to each other.

Use soft and hard edges for modelling.

Suggest texture by dry-brush or sgraffito techniques and under-paint beforehand.

Develop your experiment but do NOT overwork it.

Conclude:

Clean up.

Further thoughts:

Also continue to experiment so that the animal is totally abstract.

In other words it is just a shape within the experiment.

Continue to vary the viewpoint of your imaginary animal.

DEVELOPMENT: Extensions

In the Development extension activities:

Draw on what you have learnt.

You can link what you have learned to your own goals.

DEVELOPMENT: Extension 1

Imagine a distorted MMM image to start.

Materials:

Use the SAME materials as used in a previous experiment from Unit One.

Use the SAME MMM image as used in a previous experiment Unit One.

Begin:

BUT repeat only one of the experiments.

DEVELOPMENT: Extension 2

Imagine a semi-abstract MMM image to start.

Materials:

Use the SAME materials as used in a previous experiment from Unit Two.

Use the SAME MMM image as used in a previous experiment Unit Two.

Begin:

BUT repeat only one of the experiments.

DEVELOPMENT: Extension 3

Imagine an abstract MMM image to start.

Materials:

Use the SAME materials as used in a previous experiment from Unit Three.

Use the SAME MMM image as used in a previous experiment Unit Three.

Begin:

BUT repeat only one of the experiments.

CONGRATULATIONS.

You have taken the IMAGINATION pathway.

This is the final step to being the artist you want to be.

Your MMM experiments are like the athletes training program.

Like Olympic athletes if you want to stay at the h ghest level you keep training.

Your MMM experiments become a normal routine.

Make notes, do sketches and record what you can see.

This is material you can draw on when continuing your MMM experiments.

Make a habit of carrying a sketchpad or scraps cf paper and a pen or pencil.

Start each day with a short period of experiments.

Then move to your main artistic tasks.

You'll need to construct YOUR OWN MMM experimental programs.

By now this should not be difficult.

Planning major works could follow from that.

But do them as extensions of your MMM experiments.

A slightly larger experiment can develop into a major work.

Then much of the planning and preparatory work has been done.

WHERE NEXT?

There are other books that link with this book.
BUT they have a different focus.
You can specialize by completing ONE of the books.
But you can also complete as many of these books as you wish.
That could even be at different times.
Then you are on you way to becoming the artist YOU want to be.

Buildings
http://www.amazon.com/dp/B08CPJJTJS

Figures
http://www.amazon.com/dp/B08CPDL76B

Flowers
http://www.amazon.com/dp/B08CPLDRVT

Landscapes
http://www.amazon.com/dp/B08CPBJY1G

Portraits
http://www.amazon.com/dp/B08CPLDRW3

Still Life
http://www.amazon.com/dp/B08CPLLXRB

An Art Program is a background to these books.
The An Art Program book series can also be used to teach from.
http://www.amazon.com/dp/1731347324
hardcover book
http://www.amazon.com/dp/B09GQSNY86

NOT NOW:

Perhaps one of these books could interest you then?

Publish a book about your own memories?
http://www.amazon.com/dp/B087DWKPTP

A simple way to start developing creativity.
If you are a parent, teacher or who meet a group regularly?
http://www.amazon.com/dp/B088T1KFQZ

Start an art career.
It's NOW is harder than it ever was.
To help someone start – they download this link.
http://www.amazon.com/dp/B088T7VJ76

More of my memories
http://www.amazon.com/dp/B088Y4RPL9

SEND TO:

Know anyone interested in chocolate recipes?
Send them a link then.
http://www.amazon.com/dp/B088Y4RPL9

What about his book – Animals?
http://www.amazon.com/dp/B08CP92NMW